THE HOLOCAUST LIBRARY

The Righteous Gentiles

by

VICTORIA SHERROW

Books in the Holocaust Library

The Death Camps
The Final Solution
The Nazis
Nazi War Criminals
The Resistance
The Righteous Gentiles
The Survivors

Library of Congress Cataloging-in-Publication Data

Sherrow, Victoria.
  The righteous gentiles / by Victoria Sherrow.
    p. cm. — (The Holocaust library)
  Includes bibliographical references and index.
  Summary: Presents an overview of non-Jews throughout Europe who tried to save Jews from persecution and extermination by the Nazis.
  ISBN 1-56006-093-X (alk. paper)
  1. Righteous Gentiles in the Holocaust—Juvenile literature.
  2. World War, 1939–1945—Jews—Rescue—Juvenile literature.
  3. Holocaust, Jewish (1939–1945)—Juvenile literature.
[1. Righteous Gentiles in the Holocaust. 2. World War, 1939–1945—Jews—Rescue. 3. Holocaust, Jewish (1939–1945)] I. Title. II. Series: Holocaust library (San Diego, Calif.)
D804.65.S54 1998
364.87'81'08992404—dc21   97-36191
                                                       CIP
                                                        AC

Copyright 1998 by Lucent Books, Inc., P.O. Box 289011,
San Diego, CA 92198-9011

Table of Contents

Foreword

More than eleven million innocent people, mostly Jews but also millions of others deemed "subhuman" by Adolf Hitler such as Gypsies, Russians, and Poles, were murdered by the Germans during World War II. The magnitude and unique horror of the Holocaust continues to make it a focal point in history—not only the history of modern times, but also the entire record of humankind. While the war itself temporarily changed the political landscape, the Holocaust forever changed the way we look at ourselves.

Starting with the European Renaissance in the 1400s, continuing through the Enlightenment of the 1700s, and extending to the Liberalism of the 1800s, philosophers and others developed the idea that people's intellect and reason allowed them to rise above their animal natures and conquer poverty, brutality, warfare, and all manner of evils. Given the will to do so, there was no height to which humanity might not rise. Was not mankind, these people argued, the noblest creation of God—in the words of the Bible, "a little lower than the angels"?

Western Europeans believed so heartily in these concepts that when rumors of mass murders by the Nazis began to emerge, people refused to accept—despite mounting evidence—that such things could take place. Even the Jews who were being deported to the death camps had a hard time believing that they were headed toward extermination. Rational beings, they argued, could not commit such actions. When the veil of secrecy was finally ripped from the death camps, however, the world recoiled in shock and horror. If humanity was capable of such depravity, what was its true nature? Were humans lower even than animals instead of just beneath the angels?

The perpetration of the Holocaust, so far outside the bounds of society's experience, cried out for explanations. For more than a half century, people have sought them. Thousands of books, diaries, sermons, poems, plays, films, and lectures have been devoted to almost every imaginable aspect of the Holocaust, yet it remains one of the most difficult episodes in history to understand.

Some scholars have explained the Holocaust as a uniquely German event, pointing to the racial supremacy theories of German philosophers, the rigidity of German society, and the tradition of obedience to authority. Others have seen it as a uniquely Jewish phenomenon, the culmination of centuries of anti-Semitism in Christian Europe. Still others have said that the Holocaust was a unique combination of these two factors—a set of circumstances unlikely ever to recur.

Such explanations are comfortable and simple—too simple. The Holocaust was neither a German event nor a Jewish event. It was a human event. The same forces—racism, prejudice, fanaticism—that sent millions to the gas chambers have not disappeared. If anything, they have become more evident. One cannot say, "It can't happen again." On a different scale, it has happened again. More than a million Cambodians were killed between 1974 and 1979 by a Communist government. In 1994 thousands of innocent civilians were murdered in tribal warfare between the Hutu and Tutsi tribes in the African nations of Burundi and Rwanda. Christian Serbs in Bosnia embarked on a program of "ethnic cleansing" in the mid-1990s, seeking to rid the country of Muslims.

The complete answer to the Holocaust has proved elusive. Indeed, it may never be found. The search, however, must continue. As author Elie Wiesel, a survivor of the death camps, wrote, "No one has the right to speak for the dead. . . . Still, the story had to be told. In spite of all risks, all possible misunderstandings. It needed to be told for the sake of our children."

Each book in Lucent Books' seven volume Holocaust Library covers a different topic that reveals the full gamut of human response to the Holocaust. *The Nazis, The Final Solution, The Death Camps*, and *Nazi War Criminals* focus on the perpetrators of the Holocaust and their plan to eliminate the Jewish people. Volumes on *The Righteous Gentiles, The Resistance*, and *The Survivors* reveal that humans are capable of being "the noblest creation of God," able to commit acts of bravery and altruism even in the most terrible circumstances.

History offers a way to interpret and reinterpret the past and an opportunity to alter the future. Lucent Books' topic-centered approach is an ideal introduction for students to study such phenomena as the Holocaust. After all, only by becoming knowledgeable about such atrocities can humanity hope to prevent future crimes from occurring. Although such historical lessons seem clear and unavoidable, as historian Yehuda Bauer wrote, "People seldom learn from history. Can we be an exception?"

Chronology of Events

1933

March 23 Nazis open their first concentration camp, Dachau, outside Munich, Germany.

February–December Thousands of Jews, artists, writers, musicians, and other anti-Nazis leave Germany; refugees include Otto and Edith Frank, who flee to Holland with daughters Margot and Anne.

1935

September–November German parliament passes the Nuremberg Laws which deny Jews citizenship and various other civil rights.

1937

July 16 Buchenwald concentration camp is opened; prisoners include men who oppose Nazism, including clergy, Communists, and some Jews.

1938

March 13 Nazi troops march into Austria and declare it part of Germany; anti-Jewish decrees steadily deprive Jews of civil rights, jobs, education, and business and personal property.

May 29 Anti-Jewish laws are passed in Hungary.

July 5 Worldwide conference is held in Evian, France, to discuss the plight of German Jewish refugees; however, most nations retain quotas that limit immigration.

October 5 Passports of German Jews are stamped with a large red *J*, labeling them as different from others.

November 9–10 *Kristallnacht*—the "Night of Broken Glass": Nazis carry out a mass, violent demonstration against Jews and their homes and businesses in Germany and Austria.

November 15 Jewish children are banned from German schools.

1939

September 3 World War II begins as Poland's allies, France and Great Britain, declare war on Germany.

November 23 Jews in Poland are required to wear armbands with a yellow Star of David whenever they appear in public.

November 28 In Piotrkow, Poland, Nazis set up the first of many ghettos where they will isolate, perse-cute, and kill Jews.

1940

January–June Nazis require business owners to use Jews as slave laborers; while most employers exploit these workers, some use their positions to help.

May 1 A large Jewish ghetto is set up in Lodz, Poland.

May 10 German troops invade Holland, Belgium, and France.

June 22 France falls to the Nazis, who occupy the north; Ambassador Aristides de Sousa Mendes, Portuguese ambassador to France, defies his government's orders and issues visas to some 30,000 Jewish refugees so they can escape through Portugal.

November 15 The Warsaw Ghetto, largest of all the Jewish ghettos, is sealed.

1941

July Nazi troops enter Croatia, part of Yugoslavia, and begin deporting Jews.

September 28 A terrifying two-day massacre of Jews at Babi Yar in the Ukraine leaves 30,000 people dead and others on the run.

October Cardinal Gerlier, the archbishop of Lyons, protests anti-Jewish decrees and instructs French Catholics to help Jews.

October 15 Nazis in Poland decree that any Jew found outside the ghetto will be killed; laws state that aiding Jews is a "crime" punishable by death.

December 7 Japanese bombers attack the U.S. naval base at Pearl Harbor, Hawaii, prompting the United States to enter the war.

December 8 The first mass killings of Jews at a concentration camp begin in Chelmno in Poland.

Winter 1941–42 At Le Chambon, France, Protestant villagers led by Pastor André Trocmé begin rescue work that will save about five thousand Jews.

1942

March 1 Mass killings using gas chambers begin in the death camp Sobibor in Poland; Trainloads of Jews begin arriving at the death camp Auschwitz.

March 17 Mass killings begin at the Belzec death camp in Poland.

July Nazis carry out massive roundups of Jews in Paris and other cities in occupied France; many escapees go into hiding; in Amsterdam, Otto Frank and his family go into hiding with the help of Gentile friends.

July 22 Nazis begin deporting thousands of Jews from the Warsaw ghetto to death camps.

Summer–Fall Mussolini resists Hitler's directives to send Jews to concentration camps; he continues to let Jewish relief groups operate in Italy.

September Father Pierre Chaillet, a leader of *Amities Chretiennes* (Christian Friendship), a French organization that helps Jews, is arrested and imprisoned; other Jesuits continue his work.

October Hermann Graebe, a German-born construction engineer, witnesses massacre of Jewish civilians in Dubno, Poland; he sets out to hire Jewish workers and saves 300 lives by war's end; Norwegian rescuers smuggle about 930 Jews across the border into neutral Sweden to prevent their deportation; Nazi troops move into southern France, the "Free Zone"; Jews seek refuge in homes, convents, monasteries, and other places.

1943

March Rescuer Gertrude Luckner is convicted of treason and sent to the Ravensbrück concentration camp in Germany.

May Members of the Bulgarian parliament, church leaders, and the public protest Nazi plans to deport Bulgarian Jews; Jews are allowed to remain in Old Bulgaria.

September In Assisi, Bishop Nicolini asks Father Rufino Niccacci to form a rescue group; the "Assisi Underground" consists of priests, nuns, and Catholic lay-people; in Genoa, Pietro Cardinal Boetto and Father Francesco Repetto organize nuns, monks, and priests to rescue Jews and take over work that had been done by Delasem, a Jewish relief organization; in Poland, Irene Gut (Opdyke) is forced to watch a public hanging of Jews and the Gentiles who had helped them; she continues to hide Jews.

October Oskar Schindler convinces Nazi officials to let him transport 1,100 Jewish workers from Poland to his new factory in the former Czech Republic, thus saving them from death.

October 2 Danish citizens launch mass rescue effort to help 7,000 Jews escape to neutral Sweden before they can be deported.

October 16 Nazis launch what is later called the "Black Sabbath" raid in Rome; thousands of Jews go into hiding.

1944

May–June After taking control in Hungary, Nazis send about 400,000 Hungarian Jews to their deaths in Auschwitz-Birkenau.

June Swedish diplomat Raoul Wallenberg arrives in Hungary to lead rescue mission financed by U.S. War Refugee Board; his efforts will save more than 100,000 Hungarian Jews.

August 4 In Amsterdam, Nazis find and arrest the Frank family; only Otto Frank will survive the war.

August 11 Dutch rescuer Joop Westerweel is executed by the Nazis.

December Ellen Nielsen, a Danish widow who helped to rescue at least 100 Jews, is arrested and sent to a Nazi concentration camp; she survives the war.

1945

January 17 Soviet agents arrest Raoul Wallenberg in Budapest and imprison him; his fate remains unknown as of 1997.

April 30 Adolf Hitler commits suicide.

May 8 Germany surrenders to the Allies.

November 22 Nazi war crimes trials begin in Nuremberg.

1953

August Israeli parliament passes Martyrs' and Heroes' Remembrance Law; Yad Vashem, the Martyrs' and Heroes' Remembrance Authority, is authorized to recognize Righteous Gentiles.

1957

November 6 Holocaust survivors and their rescuers meet in New York City to help dedicate a memorial to "Christian Heroes who helped their Jewish Brethren escape the Nazi terror" erected by the Anti-Defamation League of the B'nai B'rith; Soviet officials announce that Raoul Wallenberg died in prison in 1947; yet, people claim they saw him in various prisons and hospitals as late as the 1970s.

1988

Psychologists Sam and Pearl Oliner publish results of their long-term study comparing the traits of rescuers versus bystanders in Nazi Europe.

1993

Steven Spielberg's film *Schindler's List* tells the story of rescuer Oskar Schindler as it reveals the horrors of the Holocaust.

Choosing Goodness

On July 16, 1942, the people of Paris awoke to see German trucks stopping abruptly on streets throughout their city. Nazi police proceeded to enter apartment buildings, their heavy boots stomping on the stairs. Going door to door, they knocked sharply and ordered residents to let them inside.

It became clear that the Nazis were rounding up men, women, and children, loading them onto the trucks, and taking them away. People waited in terror as Nazi search teams approached their homes. One of these frightened people was seven-year-old Odette Meyers. At 5:00 that morning, Meyers and her mother had been awakened by the apartment manager, a middle-aged woman named Marie Chotel whom Odette called "Madame Marie." Meyers later recalled:

> She ran up, yanked us out of bed and said, "They are coming for you!" She threw us quickly into her apartment and put us, my mother and me, into a broom closet and closed the door. . . . The search team came in, and Madame Marie immediately, with all her peasant shrewdness, put on a terrific act.[1]

Madame Chotel poured glasses of wine for the Nazis and chatted with them in a friendly way while Odette and her mother hid in the closet, fearing for their lives. The men were convinced that the Meyers family was somewhere in the building, and they threatened to search for them. They told Chotel she would suffer the same fate as the Jews if she was lying about the Meyers's whereabouts. Chotel calmly insisted that the family had gone to stay in the country. In the end, the Nazis believed her and left empty-handed. The Meyerses were safe—for the moment.

Why were Odette Meyers and her mother forced to hide, pursued ruthlessly by police who planned to send them to their deaths? And why did Marie Chotel have to fear for her life because she was helping them?

In ordinary times, innocent men, women, and children do not expect to be hunted down like criminals. People who help others are admired for showing kindness and compassion. But these were not ordinary times. These were years in which someone could be hanged for sheltering an old man or shot for feeding a hungry child. During these years, men received job promotions and praise for seizing terrified families and killing unarmed women and children. These were years of unreasoning evil, the years of Adolf Hitler and the Nazis.

A Twisted World

For twelve long years, from 1933 to mid-1945, the Jews of Europe were persecuted, then targeted for death because they had been born into a particular religion. Their oppressors were the Nazis—National Socialists—led by the German dictator Adolf Hitler.

The Nazis began as a small, radical political party that slowly gained strength during the 1920s, a time of economic depression and political unrest. Germany had been humiliated by its defeat in World War I (1914–1918). The Versailles treaty of 1919 punished Germany for starting the destructive war, which led to 10 million deaths. The victorious Allied nations forced Germany to reduce its military, give up territory in France and Poland, and pay billions of dollars in damages.

In his speeches and writings, Nazi leader Adolf Hitler bitterly condemned these terms and the German officials who accepted them, and appealed to the hurt pride of the German people. He claimed pure Germans, or Aryans, were a superior race destined to rule over others and expand their territory in Europe. Hitler promised political stability and work for the millions of jobless.

Along with solutions to Germany's problems, Hitler offered people a scapegoat. For years he had expressed intense hatred toward Jews. Although Jews comprised less than 1 percent of the population, the Nazis claimed that they had caused Germany's defeat in World War I and numerous other problems,

Adolf Hitler with admirers in 1926, one year after he wrote the autobiographical Mein Kampf.

including the economic depression. Hitler disregarded the fact that one hundred thousand Jews had fought for Germany and twelve thousand had died in the war. He called Jews "parasites" who had destroyed German culture, ignoring their many contributions to science, music, literature, art, commerce, and other achievements.

In his 1925 autobiographical tract *Mein Kampf* (*My Struggle*) and in many of his speeches, Hitler expressed a desire to make Germany *Judenrein*—free of Jews. When the Nazis swept into power in 1933, he put these plans in motion. The Nazis unleashed a vast propaganda campaign designed to build support for their regime and to stir up anti-Semitism, or hatred or discrimination toward Jews. Such prejudice had ancient roots in Germany and other nations. Non-Jewish Germans were encouraged to avoid all contact with Jews and to express hostility toward them. They were told that until Jews were rendered powerless, then eliminated from the country, Germany could not gain its "proper" place among nations.

Anti-Jewish policies soon became law, enforced by the totalitarian police state that the Nazis created. The full force of government was used to persecute the half million Jews who lived in Germany. By the end of 1935, Jews had lost their civil rights and been ousted from numerous jobs and professions. Within three years, the Nazis had seized Jewish businesses and other property and banned them from public parks, pools, theaters, and other places. Young Jews could no longer attend school or universities. Jews were required to carry identity cards marked with a large black *J*. Groups of Nazi thugs called storm troopers harassed and attacked them on the street. In a multitude of ways, German Jews were isolated, humiliated, terrorized, and impoverished.

A 1935 German road sign reads, "Jews Are Uninvited Guests." By the end of this year, Jews in Germany had already lost most of their civil rights.

At first, many Jews did not take Hitler seriously. This was their country, too; they were also Germans. They believed their fellow citizens would reject Hitler and that common sense would prevail over irrational hatred. But as their plight worsened, thousands of Jews lost hope and fled Germany. By 1938 nearly 130,000 Jews had emigrated; another 35,000 left that year.

Throughout 1938 Jews sought to leave Germany and also Austria, which Germany had annexed in March. That fall, part of Czechoslovakia also came under Nazi control, further expanding Hitler's Reich, or empire. More violence occurred against Jews and their property, including a brutal nationwide attack on the night of November 9. About thirty thousand Jews were arrested and sent to forced labor or concentration camps, where the Nazis detained people they wished to punish or subdue, political opponents and other "asocials" as well as Jews.

Only a small percentage of those who wished to leave could obtain legal permits to immigrate to England, the United States, and other countries throughout the world whose laws limited the number of people who could enter each year. A worldwide economic depression had led most nations to lower the number of refugees they would accept. Poor refugees were especially unwelcome, and the Nazis let Jewish emigrants take only about ten dollars with them.

The number of Jews facing the Nazi threat soared in 1939 as country after country fell to Germany's efficient war machine. In September the rest of Czechoslovakia and all of Poland crumbled in the onset of World War II. The next year, Germany attacked and occupied Norway, Denmark, Luxembourg, Belgium, the Netherlands, and France. Turning back to eastern Europe, its armies swept into Lithuania, Romania, and the vast territories of the Soviet Union, their former ally, in 1941.

A Fight for Survival

As German troops subdued nations throughout western and eastern Europe, the Nazis used new and more brutal methods in their other war against the Jewish people. During 1940 and 1941, Hitler authorized the formation of killing squads in eastern Europe. These units marched large groups of Jews from towns and villages to wooded, rural areas where they were shot and buried in mass graves. The Nazis also tested and used poison gas to kill people inside sealed vans, which were moved from place to place. Many thousands of Jews died of disease, starvation, exposure to cold, and Nazi bullets or bayonets after they were forced into crowded, walled-off ghettos in Warsaw and many other cities.

However, the Nazis decided that emigration, ghettos, and killing squads were not fast or "efficient" enough ways to get rid of Jews. They devised a secret plan, referred to as the "final solution of the Jewish question." As 1942 began, Jews of all ages in conquered territory were targeted for death. The Nazis arranged mass deportations of ghetto residents. Aided by local collaborators, they began rounding up the remaining Jews for shipment to extermination camps, isolated in occupied Poland.

In a photograph taken by a German soldier and enclosed in a letter home in 1942, a German police officer fires at a Jewish mother and child after other Jews have dug their own mass grave.

In 1933, 8 million Jews and about 300 million non-Jews (Gentiles) lived in Europe. When World War II ended, a shocked world learned that 6 million Jews, along with 5 million non-Jewish civilians, had been killed by the Nazis. Jews had endured unimaginable horrors in death factories such as Auschwitz-Birkenau in Poland. At this camp alone, more than a million men, women, and children had been gassed to death. Then their bodies were burned in massive ovens designed for that purpose. These mass murders, part of the deliberate plan to wipe out an entire people, came to be known as the Holocaust.

Taking a Stand

During the Holocaust, non-Jews faced important moral choices and followed different paths. Some became perpetrators, personally committing acts of persecution from harassment to murder. Others collaborated with the German forces charged with carrying out such crimes, either for material gain, out of fear, or because they agreed with Nazi ideas. Many people exploited the situation for personal gain. They looted the homes of Jews who had been taken away, "bought" their businesses or other possessions for unfairly low prices, or blackmailed people in hiding by threatening to inform on them. Some spoke against Nazism or actively resisted the Nazis. The vast majority of Europeans were bystanders who got through those years as best they could, focusing on the welfare of themselves and their families.

Then there were people who reached out to help Jews, in some cases to save their lives. These rescuers were the smallest group of all. About 1 million Jews managed to escape from Nazi Germany and the lands it invaded and occupied; another million

survived in those lands until the war ended. Holocaust historians have said that the Jews who survived were aided by at least one non-Jew.

Aid took various forms. Rescuers hid Jews, helped them to escape, provided forged identity papers, and supplied food, clothing, ration coupons, and other needs. Some people helped from time to time in ways that involved little risk. They might offer food, money, or clothing to someone in need, distract police who were hunting for Jews, or warn people when danger loomed. Other non-Jews gave sustained help, in some cases for one or more years. Some people took dramatic actions to save lives. Others performed many routine tasks, meeting the day-to-day needs of Jews in hiding.

Aware that people were being persecuted and killed, these individuals felt compelled to act. Author and Holocaust survivor Elie Wiesel has said, "Each and every one of them is a reminder of what so many others could have done, of what so many others did not do."[2]

"I Could Not Stand Idly By"

Who were these people who held fast to the highest human values during the darkest of times? Rescuers lived in every country under Nazi rule and came from all economic and social classes and professions. Some worked alone, others as part of organized or informal networks who cooperated to save lives. They belonged to different religious groups or to none at all, and had grown up in different kinds of families.

Some rescuers helped friends, relatives, or acquaintances. Others were quite willing to help strangers. Most began their rescue activities because someone asked for their help; a smaller number sought out opportunities to rescue people.

"Righteous Among the Nations"

In August 1953, the Israeli Parliament passed the Martyrs' and Heroes' Remembrance Law, instituting Yad Vashem, the Martyrs' and Heroes' Remembrance Authority. As a center for research on the Holocaust, Yad Vashem contains a museum, library, and numerous historical materials and artifacts.

Yad Vashem was also authorized to identify and honor Righteous Gentiles, defined as "high-minded Gentiles who risked their lives to save Jews" during the Holocaust. To be designated a Righteous Gentile, a person must have helped to save the life of one or more Jews during the period of Nazi persecution in Europe, without having done so for material gain. The individual's behavior must surpass ordinary help, which Yad Vashem agrees is also praiseworthy. Beyond refusing to do evil, he or she must have taken positive action in spite of attendant risks or hardships.

As of mid-1997, 13,700 Righteous Gentiles had been recognized by Yad Vashem. In honor of each individual, a carob tree is planted along the Avenue of the Righteous in Jerusalem or on a terraced hillside located beyond the plaza near the Holocaust Museum. A plaque on the tree shows the name and nationality of the honored person. Righteous Gentiles also receive a certificate and the Yad Vashem medal. On the front of the medal is engraved an arm reaching up through barbed wire toward a globe; the other side features a view of Yad Vashem. Inscribed on the medal are these words: "Whoever saves a single soul, it is as if he had saved the whole world."

The medal awarded to Righteous Gentiles by Yad Vashem is engraved with the words, "Whoever saves a single soul, it is as if he had saved the whole world."

While rescuers were outwardly different, they shared certain traits. They were willing to take risks, able to think and act quickly, and flexible enough to adjust their lives in order to help others. After interviewing more than one hundred rescuers from different countries, author Malka Drucker and photographer Gay Block concluded that these people shared "an open heart" and tended to think for themselves, as individuals. Drucker and Block found rescuers had "a streak of rebelliousness and nonconformity . . . an adventurous spirit."[3] Some firmly believed that their moral principles were worth dying for. As one Danish clergyman said, "I would rather die with the Jews than live with the Nazis."[4]

Living in a world in which right and wrong seemed to have no meaning, these people held fast to their inner values. They saw injustice and took action. Yet most rescuers claim they did nothing special or unusual, just what anyone would have done under the circumstances. One rescuer, for example, stated, "If you can save somebody's life, that's your duty";[5] another said, "I could not stand idly by and observe the daily misery that was occurring."[6]

Called heroes by others, rescuers often scoff at this label. Typical is this response: "I do not feel I am a hero. I feel that I only did my duty."[7] Dutch rescuer Johtje Vos has said simply: "We did it because we believed it was the right thing to do."[8]

For some time, rescuers received little attention and many of them preferred it that way. As facts about the Holocaust became known, a stunned world tried to comprehend the vast brutality and systematic mass murder that had occurred. Most researchers and authors focused on the perpetrators and their victims. Survivors struggled to rebuild their lives.

In recent decades, however, rescuers have been increasingly recognized and honored by Jews and Gentiles alike. Jewish leaders and writers are among those who have urged that their stories be told. Sholem Asch writes, "Let the epic of heroic deeds of love, as opposed by those of hatred, of rescue as opposed to destruction, bear equal witness to unborn generations."[9]

In Israel, rescuers became known as *Hasidei Umot HaOlam*, Hebrew for "Righteous Among the Nations of the World." Here, then, are some of their stories, inspiring accounts of courage and compassion. These are the people who could not stand by. Against a backdrop of evil and indifference, risking their very lives, they chose goodness.

Righteous Gentiles in Hitler's Germany

After Hitler seized power in Germany in 1933, his government made hatred and persecution the law of the land. Stiff punishment awaited those who mingled with or helped Jews, of whom about 170,000 remained in Germany when World War II began in 1939. By that time, it was extremely difficult to leave Germany; by 1941, it was virtually impossible. Jews found themselves trapped in Nazi Germany as Hitler and his top aides began implementing the murderous Final Solution.

During the 1930s, the Nazis crushed German opposition and voices of protest steadily dwindled. Dissenters risked arrest and interrogation, often accompanied by beatings, confinement in one of hundreds of concentration camps for "re-education," or perhaps death. Among the "crimes" for which someone could be put to death was telling jokes about Hitler.

Yet even in Germany, surrounded by millions of Nazi Party members and supporters, rigid laws, police, and informers, some people refused to cooperate. They rejected the endless stream of anti-Jewish propaganda and recognized Jews as human beings like themselves, people who desperately needed help. When the war ended, about twenty-five thousand German Jews had survived. Some of them had been aided by organized groups, but most were saved by individuals.

"You Had to Be Aware": Gitta Bauer

Gitta Bauer grew up in Berlin, Germany, in a Catholic family that opposed Hitler. In 1929, as she and her father watched a Nazi parade, Mr. Bauer told ten-year-old Gitta, "These are people who *want* another war."[10] When she heard anti-Semitic propaganda, Gitta asked her father, "What are Jews?" He replied, "Jews are people like you and me only with a different religion."[11]

However, even Bauer was enticed by the excitement the Nazis created during the 1936 Summer Olympic Games in Berlin. Along with thousands of other teenagers, she took part in the dramatic opening ceremonies and felt a surge of German patriotism. When she told a priest about these feelings, he cautioned her that the Nazis were out to destroy the church and the entire nation.

Bauer witnessed Nazi terror firsthand on the night of November 9, 1938, known as *Kristallnacht*, or the Night of Broken Glass. She saw Nazis beating people in the street and destroying Jews' homes and shops. The local synagogue became a sheet of flames and the rabbi, known as a kind

Germans gaze into the broken windows of a Jewish-owned business that was destroyed during Kristallnacht.

man, was beaten and left bleeding on the street. Thugs had ripped out his beard.

Bauer's values and courage were put to the test in July 1944 when a Jewish friend of the family came to her for help. The woman's husband, a non-Jew, had refused to divorce her, as the Nazis required; he had lost his job as a result. Now their twenty-one-year-old daughter, Ilse Baumgart, was in grave danger. Ilse had managed to obtain fake identity papers and was working as a secretary for the Luftwaffe, the German air force. But recently, during the night shift, she had accidentally revealed her true feel-

ings. A coworker had awakened Ilse from a nap during her rest break to tell her that an attempt had been made to assassinate Hitler. Ilse had sleepily asked, "Is the pig dead?"[12]

At once, the woman reported Ilse to the head officer. The man confronted Baumgart and said he would have to arrest her. Then he left, saying he would return in fifteen minutes. Baumgart realized that he had given her a chance to escape, so she fled at once.

Now, her mother stood before Gitta Bauer with an urgent request: Would Bauer hide Ilse in her apartment? They did not know where else to turn. Bauer knew the risks were grave, but she also knew that unless she helped, Ilse Baumgart would be deported and probably killed. She later told author Eva Fogelman, "What else could I say but, 'I'll take her into my home'?"[13]

For nine months, Bauer hid Baumgart. She did not even tell her parents, because she felt it would be unfair to burden them with this dangerous secret. Near the end of the war, Bauer and Baumgart often went hungry, but both survived.

After the war, Bauer continued to care deeply about social problems. As a journalist, she covered the trials of Nazi war criminals at Nuremberg. She married a Jewish man who had been living in Switzerland, and their son, Andre, was born in 1950.

While living in East Berlin, Bauer and her husband once again faced oppression and tragedy. The Soviets, who then governed East Germany, accused Bauer's husband of being an American spy, and he was sent to prison. Bauer was also imprisoned, for four years. Her husband was finally freed after five years in Siberia, but died soon afterward of the ill effects of his ordeal.

Bauer resumed her career and became an award-winning journalist, speaking out against the damaging effects of intolerance and racism. She expressed strong support for the Jewish state in Israel. Bauer has taken issue with those Germans who claim they did not know what was happening to Jews during the Holocaust. During a speech in Essen, Germany, she told her audience, "Even if you did not see it with your own eyes, you had to be aware."[14]

From Nazi to Lifesaver: Oskar Schindler

One of the best-known Righteous Gentiles is Oskar Schindler, who saved more than twelve hundred Jews. His achievements have been described in the book *Schindler's List*, a British television documentary, and an acclaimed 1993 feature film.

Schindler was born in 1908 in Zwittau, then part of the Austrian empire and now part of the Czech Republic. He joined the Nazi Party in 1938. Although Schindler gradually became disenchanted with Hitler, he remained a party member. As a profiteer he focused on building a successful enamelware business and enjoying a luxurious lifestyle that included fine wines, gambling, and extramarital affairs.

During the war, Schindler's business, located in Kraków, Poland, produced field kits and mess equipment for the German army. By 1940 the Nazis required business owners to use Jews as laborers. Employers then paid

Gitta Bauer receives an award for her writing accomplishments. When a Jewish friend facing persecution turned to her for help, Bauer hid the woman in her home for months.

their so-called wages directly into Nazi coffers. As slave labor, the workers had no legal rights and were often mistreated, but Schindler did not believe in abusing people from the nearby Plaszow labor camp who worked in his factory. His workers were treated kindly and received extra food; Schindler had been known to replace a worker's broken eyeglasses or bring fruit to malnourished people.

As time passed, Schindler heard more about Nazi brutality and witnessed it first-hand in Kraków's ghetto. On June 8, 1942, he saw squads of SS men, the Nazi police force, with attack dogs beating unarmed Jews during a roundup. Men, women, and children were kicked, shoved against walls, and killed with a shot to the back of the neck. The Nazis appeared to have no shame or remorse.

Stunned by their barbaric behavior, Schindler decided to try to save as many people as he could. He later said, "No thinking person could fail to see what would happen. I was now resolved to do everything in my power to defeat the system."[15]

Schindler set out to expand his plant and add more workers, many of whom had no enamel-working skills. By winter 1942, he had 550 workers. The next year, Schindler convinced the Nazis to let prisoners from the Plaszow labor camp move to his factory grounds in nearby Zablocie. Although prisoners at Schindler's subcamp were still subject to Nazi rules, living conditions there were better. The prisoners also escaped the beatings and random murders that were perpetrated at Plaszow under its sadistic Nazi director, Amon Goeth, whom Schindler called "a lunatic."[16]

Women prisoners in Plaszow, Poland, work in the camp quarry. Oskar Schindler saved more than 1,200 workers from certain death in this camp when he managed to "recruit" them for his factory.

On the Brink of Death

In October 1944, three hundred of Oskar Schindler's workers set out by train from Poland for his new factory in Brinnlitz in Czechoslovakia. These women and girls were relieved to be leaving Kraków where they had seen unpredictable episodes of Nazi brutality, along with roundups and deportations. Many of the women were married to men who had left for Brinnlitz on an earlier train.

Their train came to a stop, and the women were told to get out. As they stepped off the platform, they were dismayed to find themselves still in Poland. The train had been mistakenly rerouted and had delivered its passengers to Auschwitz-Birkenau, the most notorious of the Nazi death camps. Here, most prisoners died within days of arrival. Instead of greeting their loved ones at the new Schindler factory, the women saw gaunt, sickly prisoners and grim barracks in a sea of mud. Smoke billowed from the chimney at the top of one building. An acrid odor pierced the cold air. They would soon learn it was the smell of burning flesh.

The women protested that they should not be here, but to no avail. They were processed as new inmates of Auschwitz. During this time, Schindler was unable to help, because he had been arrested on charges of bribing Nazi officials and dealing in the black market. When he was released from jail, he heard about the missing train and went to Auschwitz himself to try to negotiate with Nazi officials for the release of these women.

By then, these prisoners had spent fourteen terrifying days at the death camp. Then, they were once again ordered onto a train but were told nothing more. When this journey ended, they emerged to see gates enclosing what looked like another camp. The women spotted a tall man smoking a cigarette—Schindler. One of the workers, Ludmilla Pfefferberg, remembers feeling indescribable relief. In a television interview years later, another of the women tried to put her feelings into words: "He was our father, he was our mother, he was our only faith. He never let us down."

On several occasions, Schindler was suspected of wrongdoing and detained in jail. But his Nazi friends saw that he was freed. Schindler maintained their loyalty with lavish gifts—liquor, food delicacies, and bolts of fancy cloth they could send to their wives back in Germany. He would bribe and charm Nazi officials and convince them that granting his requests would help the war effort.

In 1944, as Germany faced military defeat, the Nazis escalated their attacks on Jews. They had emptied the ghetto, shot the inhabitants, and buried them in mass graves. Workers were now forced to dig up these thousands of bodies and burn them on long wooden pyres at Plaszow to prevent Allied troops from discovering the atrocity.

As the ash of burning bodies filled the air, Schindler devised a daring plan to save his workers. He promised his friend and company accountant, Itzhak Stern, "I'm going to get you out. I'm going to get you *all* out."[17]

Schindler persuaded Nazi officials to let him build a new factory in Brinnlitz, near Zwittau. He insisted that he must take along the "skilled workers" whose names he would place on a now-famous list. The Nazis demanded that the list be limited to eleven hundred names. Schindler had already paid more than forty thousand dollars just for permission to move his plant. Now, the Nazi commander told Schindler that he would only release the workers in exchange for valuable diamonds.

On October 15, eight hundred Jews, followed by hundreds more, left Plaszow on trains bound for Brinnlitz. They were safe—

they were going with Schindler. At the new camp, they found decent housing and enough to eat. Schindler convinced the Nazi guards to let him run his factory without brutality or interference. Under Schindler's direction, the workers made materials for the German army that were purposely sabotaged and thus mostly useless.

When the war ended, Schindler had used up his wealth to save lives. Fearing they would be executed by Soviet troops, Oskar and his wife, Emilie, fled to Switzerland. They carried a testimonial letter written by Jews he had helped and a gold ring they had made for him. These words from the Talmud

(Right) Oskar and Emilie Schindler. (Below) Schindler's armament factory in Brinnlitz concentration camp undergoes construction.

were etched inside: "He who saves a single life saves the world entire."

"To Love One's Neighbor": Religious Rescuers

In order to protect their own institutions in the Third Reich, the official name of Hitler's regime, many high-ranking Catholic and Protestant officials did not strongly or consistently oppose the Nazis. Some protesting clergy limited their concern to Jews who had converted to Christianity.

Clergy who did protest the persecution of Jews were usually sent to concentration camps such as Dachau, which contained a special pastors' barracks for clergymen of various faiths who had been labeled enemies of the Reich. Among them was Pastor Martin Niemöller. Niemöller had been a highly decorated submarine captain in World War I. As a clergyman, he was known as a skillful orator. When the Nazis first rose to power, he did not object, but by 1935, he was preaching sermons that challenged Hitler and his ideology. He wrote, "Anti-Semitism of the [Nazis] forces one to hate the Jews, while Christianity directs one to love one's neighbor." [18]

Niemöller organized an anti-Nazi branch of Lutheranism called the Confessional Church, which drew three thousand Protestant clergy. Another three thousand joined the anti-Nazi German Christian Faith Movement. About eleven thousand remained uncommitted. When Niemöller was arrested in 1942 and tried in a Nazi court, he declared, "I have always had the best interests of Germany at heart. Hitler is destroying our country." [19] The judge fined and released him, but the Gestapo, or secret police, arrested him again as he left the courtroom and sent him to Sachsenhausen concentration camp. Convicted of being an "antisocial parasite,"

Martin Niemöller protested Nazi actions against the Jews. Eventually, Niemöller was sent to a concentration camp for his activities.

Niemöller spent time in two concentration camps but managed to survive inhumane conditions until the war ended. He returned to Germany where he preached and wrote about the evils of the Holocaust. One of Niemöller's most often quoted pieces is an eloquent testimony to becoming involved when injustice threatens:

> First they came for the Jews, but I did not speak out—because I was not a Jew. Next they came for the Communists, but I did not speak out because I was not a Communist. Then they came for the trade unionists, but I did not speak out because I was not a trade unionist. Then they came for me—and there was no one left to speak out for me. [20]

Gertrude Luckner

Gertrude Luckner was among the leaders of the Caritas Catholica, a Catholic social service organization. At first, the group aided Christians who had converted from Judaism, but it expanded its work to help all Jews, especially children. Luckner had been a social worker before the war, and she used this job to good advantage to rescue Jews. She later recalled that she disliked the Nazis early on and took action in 1933:

> Knowing Rabbi Leo Baeck, who was a prominent rabbi in Berlin, I got from him the addresses of all Jewish institutions in Germany—the names and addresses in every town. And so I visited them, to tell them what was happening. In this way I was very much connected to the Jewish community. Then when the Nazis became more powerful, I went again from place to place to see what we could do, how we could help.[21]

Luckner helped Jews escape from Germany. By the 1940s, she was carrying out dangerous missions, taking messages and emigration money from abroad to Jews in Berlin. To people in hiding, Luckner brought ration coupons, false identity papers, and money to help them leave Germany. She personally escorted Jews from city to city, an activity that put her in continual danger.

The Gestapo became suspicious of her activities and arrested her early in 1943. Despite nine weeks of interrogation by Nazi police, Luckner refused to acknowledge that

Gertrude Luckner and companions at Yad Vashem in 1970. Luckner was sent to a concentration camp for her rescue efforts.

she was part of a rescue organization or identify others with whom she had worked. In March she was sent to the Ravensbrück concentration camp in Germany. Thousands died of disease and starvation at this rat-infested camp, built by the Nazis in 1936 to imprison women. Luckner managed to survive for two years until the war's end.

After the war, Luckner founded the *Freiburg Newsletter*, an annual publication featuring discussions among Jews and Christians. A collection of issues of the newsletter from 1945 to 1985 has been also published in book form. Luckner has said, "For years there has been hatred between Christians and Jews, and I hope that will pass."[22]

Shortly after Luckner reached East Berlin in May 1945, she received a letter from Rabbi Leo Baeck. Baeck had chosen to stay in Germany and serve his people throughout the war. He had spent two years in the Terezin concentration camp in

"Something Has to Be Done": Hermann Graebe

In October 1942, Hermann Graebe, a German-born construction engineer assigned to build a railroad facility in Dubno, Poland, witnessed a horrible massacre. Graebe later told a war crimes tribunal what he had seen that day. Nazi soldiers had forced unarmed victims of all ages to undress and step into a pit, where they were then shot. Graebe said:

> One of the most terrible things I remember seeing . . . was a father, perhaps in his fifties, with his boy, about as old as my son Friedel was at that time—maybe ten years old— beside him. They were . . . completely naked, waiting for their turn to go into the pit. The boy was crying and the father was stroking his head. . . . There were other members of the family there, too—the man's wife and an older woman, a white-haired lady who was maybe the grandmother. She was holding and cradling a child, singing to it softly. Then a soldier screamed for them to move into the pit.

Graebe said, "It was the cruelest thing I have ever seen. . . . I think I shall carry that scene directly to my grave. . . . I kept saying to myself, 'Something has to be done.'"

To save lives, Graebe used his position to hire Jewish workers for various jobs. The word spread, and Jews in hiding came to him for help. He eventually rescued more than three hundred Jews in Poland, Germany, and Ukraine, and his postwar testimony helped to convict Nazi war criminals.

After witnessing a mass slaughter of Jews by Nazi soldiers, Hermann Graebe knew he had no choice but to dedicate himself to saving Jewish lives.

A Narrow Escape: Margarete Nussbaum's Story

In December 1935, twenty-year-old Margarete Nussbaum decided to take a vacation from her job at a radio station in Cologne, Germany, where she had worked since 1932. Her coworkers did not know that Nussbaum had Jewish grandparents and was therefore banned, under new Nazi laws, from working in any branch of the media. She knew she would soon be fired. All employees had been asked to provide proof, such as certificates of Christian baptism, that they were not Jews.

Worried about her future, Nussbaum headed for a ski resort in the Bavarian Alps. As she approached the village, she was shocked to see a sign reading, "Jews enter at their own risk!" A local restaurant displayed a sign with the words: "Jews and dogs not allowed." She later told author Bernt Engelmann, "My dream of finding a last bit of sanity and decency was shattered. . . . What threw me into such despair was the poisoning of this beautiful and idyllic spot."

Nussbaum left the next morning, convinced that there was no room for her in Hitler's Germany. A friend put her in touch with Fraulein Bonse, a woman who was helping young people enroll in foreign schools. During these years, Bonse worked with a secret group that helped Jews and anti-Nazis leave Germany. She helped Nussbaum plan her departure—just in time, as it turned out. A few days before Nussbaum was due to leave, Bonse phoned her and urged her to get out of her apartment as soon as she had packed some personal items.

When Nussbaum arrived in Benrath to meet Bonse as planned, the older woman explained that the Gestapo was planning to arrest her. Someone at the radio station must have grown suspicious and denounced her to the Nazi police.

Nussbaum was taken by car to a large estate near the German-Dutch border where a baron's family helped her to reach Holland safely. There, she met a Dutch priest who gave Nussbaum a ticket to London, some money, and papers that permitted her to stay in London with the permission of the British Academic Exchange Service.

Nussbaum was touched and surprised by the kindness of these strangers. As she was leaving Germany, Nussbaum had thanked Fraulein Bonse and asked her why she would risk her life to help people she did not even know. The woman replied, "Because I don't want to be ashamed of myself when I come to stand before my God."

Czechoslovakia. In 1951, at Baeck's invitation, Gertrude Luckner became the first non-Jewish German to visit the State of Israel. The Jewish National Fund later planted a grove of trees to honor her sixtieth birthday, and a home for the aged in Jerusalem was named in her honor. Through the years, some Righteous Gentiles have been among the residents of this home, living their last years in Israel.

CHAPTER 2
Righteous Gentiles in Poland and Czechoslovakia

In 1939 the Nazis occupied both Czechoslovakia and Poland. Hitler was able to seize democratic Czechoslovakia without military invasion. His threats to destroy the Czech capital and brutalize the nation's people were enough to make President Emil Hacha surrender. Then, in September, German troops entered Poland. Their large army, equipped with powerful tanks and superior aircraft, defeated the Polish forces in less than a month.

Hitler had big plans for Poland. The Germans began ousting Poles from regions they wanted for their own "living space," and armed troops were posted all over the country. The Nazis viewed Poles as inferior beings fit only for slave labor and making war materials. Poles who could not work were killed, along with influential clergy, labor leaders, intellectuals, and others who might challenge the Nazis.

Once in Poland, the Nazis began to isolate, impoverish, and terrorize Jews. Polish Jews were the first to be ordered, in November 1939, to wear a visible Star of David in the form of an armband. Between 1939 and 1941, Jews from villages all over Poland were crammed into ghettos in Lublin, Warsaw, and other cities. Jews from Germany and neighboring countries were later taken to these ghettos, as well.

Like other people in Nazi Europe, most Poles were bystanders to the persecution, and some aided the Nazis. Poland had a history of anti-Semitism and periodic violence against Jews. Mistrust of Jews and other ethnic

German troops pause at a road sign during the invasion of Poland in 1939. Immediately after the occupation, Germans began to persecute and isolate the Polish Jews.

minorities dated back centuries, and many Jews lived apart from Christian Poles. The Nazis exploited these conditions and encouraged Poles to help them locate Jews. Informers received cash and other rewards for denouncing Jews and their rescuers. Gangs of Poles called *szmalcowniki* tracked down Jews in hiding and threatened to expose them and their protectors unless they were paid off.

The Germans set up a harsh occupation government in Poland and built the six killing centers known as death camps on Polish soil. The Nazis imposed especially harsh punishments on Poles who helped Jews. Marilla Feld recalls the risks: "We had heard of instances when not only an entire Polish family was shot, but the farm completely burned out—everything, the house, the animals, the farm equipment. The Germans so wanted to make sure that no Polish farmer would dare harbor a Jew."[23] The German terror tactics were appallingly successful: About 90 percent of the 3,300,000 Jews who lived in Poland before the war perished.

Yet non-Jews still braved the risks. Emanuel Ringelblum, who kept a detailed diary about life in the Warsaw ghetto, wrote that ghetto historians had documented "hundreds of instances, where, for many months, a Polish peasant has given shelter and food to Jewish refugees."[24] Thousands of Gentile rescuers were killed by Nazis or died in camps after being arrested, among them a cattle dealer in Lvóv named Jozefek, who hid thirty-five Jews.

Although there is no sure way to know how many Poles aided Jews during the Holocaust, historian Kazimierz Iranek-Osmecki estimates that there were at least 1 million. More than half of the Righteous Gentiles honored by Yad Vashem are Poles.

"We Are All God's Children": The Roslan Family

Alexander Roslan and his family lived about two blocks from the Warsaw ghetto. As a textile merchant, Roslan had been dealing with many Jewish customers before they were forced to move into the ghetto. He later said, "I wanted to know what had happened to my friends and customers because I heard terrible stories."[25]

Christian Poles were not allowed in the ghetto, but one of Roslan's brothers, a member of the underground, sneaked him in. Roslan found himself unable to eat or sleep as a result of the misery he witnessed there. He told his wife, Mela, that they had to do something. The couple had two young children and were also helping to support two orphans, yet they agreed to take in thirteen-year-old Jacob Gutgelt. Roslan built a false wall in a cupboard, covering it with dishes so that Jacob could hide there during Gestapo raids.

After some close calls, Roslan decided to move to a house outside the city. Soon thereafter, he was asked to take in Jacob's brother, nine-year-old Sholom. He and Mela discussed the dangers but agreed the boy could come. A crisis occurred when the children became ill with scarlet fever, and Yurek, Roslan's son, had to go to the hospital. Since Sholom, who was also sick, could not receive hospital care, Yurek took careful notes about his treatment and saved half of his medicine, which his mother took home. Even so, Sholom, who had been frail when he arrived, died. The family barely had time to adjust to that tragedy when Jacob developed a severe brain infection. Roslan searched for a doctor who would not betray them. To pay for Jacob's surgery, Roslan sold the family's home, making them temporarily homeless. The family rejoiced when the surgery succeeded and Jacob recovered.

Soon afterward, the Roslans took in Jacob's five-year-old brother, David. The family now had no steady income and lived in grave danger. Somehow they kept the children sheltered and fed. Alex Roslan took more risks selling goods in the black market and was arrested. He spent six weeks in jail until Mela was able to bribe officials to release him.

In April 1943 the last remaining inhabitants of the Warsaw ghetto rose up against German and Polish troops sent in to evacuate it. During the period of armed resistance the family spent months living with other Poles in cellars while fighting raged on the streets. Tragedy struck again when fifteen-year-old Yurek Roslan went outside to get water and was killed by German gunfire.

As the war drew to a close, the Roslans wandered toward the Russian front. For years, Alex had shown courage for the sake of the others, but during these months, he recalls feeling "scared all the time."[26] After liberation, the Roslans tried to find Jacob and David's father since none of the boys' other relatives had survived. In 1947 the two boys joined their father in Palestine after having lived with the Roslans for four and a half years.

This photo of Jacob, David, and Sholom Gutgelt with their Aunt Janke was taken in the Warsaw ghetto before the children were smuggled out to live with the Roslans. The Roslans hid the boys despite the peril to themselves and their own son.

Alex Roslan recalls how the Gutgelt boys were first brought to him by their aunt:

> [She] said, "Please, tell me I can trust you, because we do not know you." I said, "Trust me." And they trusted me, like we had become one family. When Sholom died, when Jacob was sick, my wife thought we would not survive. I said, "Mela, if I lost everything, I will not break my promise."[27]

The Roslan family made enormous sacrifices to keep that promise, but Alex has said he would do it again. The compassion he expressed during those years took root in childhood when he saw his parents and other relatives actively helping people in need and heard his grandmother often say, "We are all God's children."[28]

Alex Roslan poses with David and Jacob Gutgelt, the two Jewish children he rescued. Although the Roslans also hid brother Sholom, he died of scarlet fever while under their care.

"Little Miracles"

One cold winter afternoon in 1943, soon after her family had been forced into the Lvóv ghetto in Poland, eight-year-old Nelly Landau went into hiding. For days, she had seen Nazis rounding up people—old people, women, children—who never returned. During a bitter storm, her mother slipped Nelly out of the ghetto to the other side of town and she moved in with a Catholic family named Krajterowa.

Nelly Landau Toll later wrote, "I felt lonely and unhappy . . . but *Pani* Krajterowa opened her arms and hugged me. She told me that she liked me and that I was now to become Marysia, her niece from a small and distant village."[29] Nelly remained with this family for a few months but returned to her parents when a boarder at the house became suspicious.

Desperate times followed. Nelly and her parents joined a group of people who had paid a German major to take them to Hungary. But the major left them stranded in a barn near the border, then disappeared. After barely escaping Nazi killing squads, the group was forced to return to the ghetto. During these grim days, Nelly was often encouraged by her beloved Grandpa Henryk, who told her, "There are always little miracles, even when hope has vanished."[30]

In spring 1943, Nelly and her mother secured a hiding place with a middle-aged couple named Wojtek, whose two-room apartment had an emergency hiding space built inside the bedroom wall. While in hiding, the two had to stay indoors, never moving about or using the toilet unless someone else was home. But Mrs. Wojtek was kind and thoughtful. She asked a friend to bring Nelly books, a diary, and watercolor paints and paper to help pass the time. (In later years, the vivid paintings she created, showing a child's visions of a happier life, were exhibited around the world.)

There were narrow escapes as the Nazis conducted random searches and neighbors paid unexpected visits. In her book *Behind the Secret Window*, Toll describes these heart-stopping raids. One of them began with a sharp knock on the door:

Mama and I froze. *Pani* Krysia locked our bedroom door, and almost immediately the police were in the kitchen. . . . Mama grabbed my hand and squeezed it hard. . . . My heart was beating so loud that I worried they might hear it. I did not dare to move. In the kitchen, we could hear an angry man ordering *Pani* Krysia to let him into the bedroom. Then someone tried to open the locked door. I watched, frozen, as the knob turned.[31]

The police demanded that Mrs. Wojtek open the door, but she insisted that her husband, who was not at home, had the key. As Nelly and her mother held each other tightly, crouching in terror, the men told Mrs. Krysia that she must find the key at once. She pretended to look for it, suggesting that the men return another time when her husband was home. The men finally agreed, but did not come back.

Another time, near the end of the war, Mr. Wojtek was smoking a cigarette near a window. The Gestapo arrested him on suspicion of sending secret signals to the enemy.

Jews in the Lvóv ghetto of Poland. When she was eight years old, Nelly Landau Toll's mother found a hiding place for her outside the ghetto after it became clear that Jews were being deported to their deaths.

Organized to Help: The Zegota

A number of Poles worked to save Jews through an organized group called the Zegota, or Rada Pomocy Zydom (Council for Aid to Jews). Catholic intellectuals led by author Zofia Kossak-Szczucka created the Zegota near the end of 1942. They worked with the Polish underground, with Jewish and Polish resistance groups, and members of anti-Fascist political parties. The group began in Warsaw then moved to other large cities—Lvóv, Kraków, Lublin.

The Zegota received funds from the exiled Polish government and foreign Jewish organizations. Individuals could turn to them for food, hiding places, transportation, and medical care. The Zegota council office also forged identification papers, labor cards, and baptismal and marriage certificates, providing dozens of these documents free on a daily basis. Even with false papers, though, most Jews living among Christians could not risk taking a job, so they needed ongoing financial help.

A report issued by the Zegota in 1943, quoted in *He Who Saves One Life*, described efforts to aid ghetto fighters and other Jews during this busy period:

> It is a nightmare—the difficulty of sheltering some of them in the forests, some in Warsaw. . . . A number of party leaders and members of the Jewish National Committee are also getting across to the Aryan side; these have to be found safe shelter in an atmosphere of terrible terror and intimidation of the population. Civilians too are managing to escape from the ghetto hell through sewers and various gaps; these too have to be looked after; we have to find shelter, provide them with forged documents, find clothing, give them money.

It is estimated that the Zegota saved more than twenty-five hundred Jewish children by hiding them with willing families or in shelters, hospitals, orphanages, or institutions run by local government or the Polish Red Cross. The group also helped four thousand others hide or escape by providing false documents and other assistance.

A typical false identity card made by the Zegota. This card was issued in Warsaw in 1942.

Again, Nelly and her mother escaped detection when police searched the apartment. One day in 1944, Mrs. Wojtek was horrified to find the words "Jews are hiding here" written in white chalk on her kitchen door. But the Wojteks continued to hide the Landaus and all four of them lived to see Soviet troops liberate their region in July 1944.

"The Children . . . Have Their Life": Tony Kalina

Thanks to Czech Antonin (Tony) Kalina, thirteen hundred children imprisoned at Buchenwald concentration camp escaped death. Kalina, a Communist, was arrested as a political subversive in 1939 at age thirty-seven. After spending time in various camps, he arrived at Buchenwald in the summer of 1944. Political prisoners were often chosen as block leaders, and Kalina was assigned to lead Block 66. In this role, he was expected to enforce camp policies among his group of prisoners.

At once, Kalina saw ways to save lives. Aided by Dr. Jindrich Flusser and other prisoners, he managed to gather more than one thousand male Jewish children and young males from various countries into his block. These boys ranged in age from three-and-a-half to sixteen. He then devised schemes to keep them from being sent to the gas chambers. At this late stage in the war, the Allies were bombing Germany and the Buchenwald camp was less well organized than before. Kalina was able to change the names of the children on various lists and thus confuse the Nazis about their real identities. He hung quarantine signs on the door to scare the Nazis into thinking the children were infected with typhoid fever.

Inside the block, Kalina and other men taught their group history and other subjects. They found ways to bring in extra food. A German Communist whom Kalina had

A six-year-old orphan stands for roll call at the Buchenwald camp. One Righteous Gentile, Antonin Kalina, was able to hide 1,300 children at Buchenwald, saving them from certain death.

known in a previous camp was also at Buchenwald. This man headed the camp store and helped Kalina get the food, clothing, and medicine he needed for those in his block.

Near the war's end, confusion at the camp allowed Kalina to substitute the files of living children for others who had died. This kept the Nazis from searching for them. Kalina recalled:

Toward the end, near Liberation, a high SS came to me and asked, "Where are your Jews?" I said, "I have no Jews here. The Jews I had yesterday went out on a transport. Here I have only children." One of my fellow prisoners asked how I could be so brave. I told him, "My life is past, but the children, they have their life before them. We saved all 1,300 boys. We all marched out of the camp after Liberation."[32]

On the Move

Jews often kept one step ahead of their pursuers, hiding in homes, institutions, farm buildings, even outdoors. During the war years, they might be sheltered by several different Gentiles.

At age six, Rose Silberberg's family left the Srodula ghetto in Poland. Stanislawa Cicha had agreed to let them hide in a chicken coop attached to her tiny home near Srodula. The floor of the coop contained a small bunker concealed by a trap door that they covered with barrels of potatoes. During part of 1943, the Silberbergs moved between the ghetto and the coop, whichever seemed safer, but they had to endure raids in both places. The Gestapo succeeded in finding them during a raid in 1944. Mrs. Cicha and some of Rose's relatives were arrested at the coop and taken to Auschwitz. In the meantime, Rose and her Aunt Sara, who were not there at the time, were able to obtain false identity papers. They moved to a German convent where they worked as servants until liberation. They were relieved to learn that Mrs. Cicha survived, too.

Jacques Van Dam of Holland first lived outside Amsterdam with the Koelewyn family. In summer 1943, Germans began raiding this area, so he left and a forester hid him for several days. Van Dam then moved to northern Holland and stayed with the Bootsma family. At various times, he hid in a bunker in the floor of their home or in their bakery. For a few months, he slept on a small barge that belonged to their relatives. When Nazis began patrolling the lakes, he slept in haylofts.

Cecile and Anny Rojer of Belgium spent their first night in hiding at the home of a Gentile friend of their parents. They spent a few months in the contagion ward of a local nursing home, then moved to a country estate where a baron and baroness were housing children from war-torn cities. Next, they were taken to the Convent of Pity, where they were shielded with other Jewish children until the war ended. The girls later recalled that one nun, Sister Clotilde, was especially kind. At night, she would say to each of them in Yiddish, "Sleep well, my child."

A Jewish woman climbs out of a concealed hiding place. Jews were not only forced to hide for long periods of time in cramped, airless quarters, they had to be able to escape at a moment's notice.

Young survivors at Buchenwald after liberation in 1945. The sight of small children such as these moved many Righteous Gentiles to try to save their lives.

A Valiant Teenager: Stefania Podgorska Burzminski

In 1941, sixteen-year-old Stefania Podgorska had more burdens than most teenagers. Living in war-torn occupied Poland, she supported herself and her six-year-old sister, Helena. Her father had died, her older siblings had moved away, and her mother and brother had been taken to Germany for forced labor. But Stefania had Jewish friends in the ghetto, and she began sneaking food to them. The more she saw, the more upset she felt. At night, she heard anguished screams as people were dragged away. She decided to assume terrifying new responsibilities. In her small apartment, she hid Joe Diamant, the son of the owners of the shop where Stefania once worked.

Joe's brother Henek and his wife also needed a refuge outside the ghetto before they were taken away. Stefania knew she could hide them, too, if she had more space. Finding a new home was unlikely in the overcrowded city, but she kept looking. She later recalled her search in a deserted section of the city:

> I didn't know where to go. Everything was empty, and I was scared. It was so ghostly. And then—you will laugh when I say this, really—then I heard a voice. I heard a voice. While I stood there thinking, asking, "Dear God, where am

I supposed to go now to look for an apartment? Where?" . . .

And then I heard the voice. Some voice told me, "Don't be afraid. Go a little farther. After this corner, two women are standing, women who clean the street. They are supporting themselves on their brooms. Ask them for an apartment. They will tell you."[33]

To her surprise, two women with brooms were standing on the next block. They directed her to a two-room cottage with a kitchen and attic, well suited to her needs, and Stefania arranged to move in. Within a short time, as more Jews fled from the ghetto, she was hiding thirteen people there along with herself and her sister. For two years, while working hard at a factory, Stefania managed to house and feed these people and keep them safe from patrolling Nazis and from two blackmailers who knew she was hiding Jews.

A new crisis occurred shortly before the war ended. The Germans set up a hospital across the street and took over nearby homes for their own use. One day, they ordered Stefania to vacate her house in two hours. As she had done before, she prayed for guidance. This time, she heard a woman's voice:

It was so beautiful, so nice, so quiet. She said to me, "Don't worry. Everything will be all right. You will not leave your apartment. You will stay here, and they will take only one room. . . . Send all your people to the bunker. Open the door. Open the windows. Clean your apartment and sing."[34]

Stefania told the thirteen people to hide in the attic and did as the voice had instructed. Neighbors came to warn her the Germans would kill her if she did not leave at once, but she refused. When the SS men arrived, they told her they would only need one room. Incredibly, for eight months, the two Nazis and their nurse girlfriends lived in the same house and did not discover the Jews in the attic.

Author Eva Fogelman, who describes Podgorska's amazing bravery in her book *Conscience and Courage*, writes, "Thirteen men, women, and children are alive today because a teenager believed in miracles."[35]

Righteous Gentiles in the Baltics and Ukraine

Not far from Poland, nearly 2 million Jews lived in the Soviet Ukraine and the Baltic countries of Lithuania, Estonia, and Latvia. In 1939, Hitler had made a pact that gave the Soviet Union control over these areas. Jews who lived inside the Russian zone were not abused as badly as they were in Nazi-occupied areas. But in 1941, Hitler attacked Russia, bent on conquering this huge country and controlling its land, people, and natural resources. Jews in the conquered territory now faced the same horrors of Nazi occupation.

Anti-Semitism was longstanding and intense throughout this region. When the Germans arrived, they fueled anti-Jewish prejudices and aroused anger through propaganda and scapegoating. They also promised the people land and power in exchange for supporting the Nazi regime. Many locals helped Nazi strike forces round up and murder Jews, as well as Communists, often in mass killings that wiped out entire villages.

Some people remained immune to Nazi ideology and the waves of hatred. Among them were brave clergy like Archbishop Szeptycki.

"The Sanctity of Man": Andreas Szeptycki

When the Nazis arrived, Andreas Szeptycki was the leader of the Ukrainian Greek Catholic Church in Galicia, a Polish-Ukrainian region, and archbishop of the department, or district, of Lvóv. A man of strong convictions, Szeptycki was in his seventies at the time of the Nazi invasion. A scholar, Archbishop Szeptycki was well traveled and spoke several languages, including Hebrew.

Ukrainians drag a Jew away to either forced deportation or execution during a pogrom, possibly in Lvóv, Poland. Many Ukrainians were anti-Semitic and readily cooperated with the Nazis.

Although the archbishop was in poor health and was confined to a wheelchair, he began speaking out at once against the Germans. Szeptycki soon realized that the Nazis and local collaborators were murdering thousands of Jews—a total of one hundred thousand in Lvóv alone.

The archbishop condemned the Nazis' actions through a pastoral letter titled "Thou Shalt Not Murder!" All priests were required to read this message to their congregations. Szeptycki also announced that religious services were closed to people who supported the murderous policies of the Nazis. Appalled at the massacres of Galician Jews in November 1942, Szeptycki declared that those who took part in these crimes would be banned from the sacraments of the church. He warned his followers that God would surely punish people who "shed innocent blood and make of themselves outcasts of human society by disregarding the sanctity of man." [36]

Szeptycki bravely confronted Nazi officials who threatened him with arrest. He wrote numerous angry letters to Nazi officials protesting their practice of ordering local people to round up and murder Jews.

Behind the Germans' backs, Szeptycki began hiding people inside the church, often disguising them as priests or nuns. Among the adults he saved was Rabbi David Kahane, who later served as the chief rabbi of the Polish army. Szeptycki hid an additional 150 people in convents. Many were children whose parents had been killed by the Nazis. Szep-

tycki also saved Torah scrolls that were precious to the Jewish community for repatriation after the war.

Heroism in Lithuania: Anna Simaite

Anna Simaite of Riga, a teacher and literary critic, was the director of the cataloguing department at Vilna University library when the war began. This quiet, scholarly woman became one of the most determined rescuers of Jews during the Holocaust.

Simaite was appalled when she saw Nazis forcing Jews into the Vilna ghetto. Trapped behind stone walls and barbed wire, twenty-five thousand people were crowded into the city blocks of five streets. These men, women, and children struggled to survive day by day. There was not nearly enough food, and ghetto dwellers lacked warm clothing, medicines, running water, and decent sanitary facilities. Children cried

A Lithuanian collaborator seems to proudly proclaim his Nazi sympathies as he leads a forced labor detachment of Jews from the Vilna ghetto. Note the white badges emblazoned with the letter J on the men's breasts.

Spiritual Life Amid the Horror

Some rescuers helped Jews to practice their religion in hiding. In a farm near Vilna, the Raczynski family had been sheltering people who managed to escape from the ghetto or evade the Nazi executions in a nearby forest. One of those who stayed with this family later told authors Gay Block and Malka Drucker about a special night when twenty Jews were then hiding in the house and barn:

> Stefan's mother prepared for us a ceremonial dinner for Chanukah [a Jewish holiday]. She put colored carpets on the floor, and we all sat together, twenty Jews, and ate, drank, and sang in Polish, Yiddish, and Hebrew. And Stefan guarded the yard so no stranger would approach the house.

Some of the priests who hid children also helped them to maintain their faith and customs. In Namur, Belgium, Father Joseph Andre taught the houseful of children under his care about Judaism. He also helped them to celebrate a traditional seder, or ceremonial meal, for the spring holiday of Passover. Others encouraged their charges to read the Torah and recite their traditional prayers. Many priests in Italy also reassured those they hid that they would not pressure them to change their religion.

In Ukraine, Archbishop Andreas Szeptycki of the Greek Catholic Church told Itzhak Lewin: "I want you to be a good Jew. . . . I am saving you for your people. I do not expect any reward, nor do I expect you to accept my faith."

out in hunger, begging for a piece of bread, a potato, or a turnip. People died on the streets. Their bodies were covered with newspapers until a wooden cart arrived to remove them.

When she realized what was being done to these people, Simaite was determined to act. She later told author Philip Friedman, "I could no longer go on with my work. I could not remain in my study. I could not eat. I was ashamed."[37] What could she do to help? Non-Jews were banned from entering the ghetto; most were also afraid to go there. Simaite devised a plan to get in. She convinced German officials that the ghetto contained valuable books that she must recover for the university library. From then on, she spent hours, even days, inside the ghetto, smuggling messages, food, flowers, and sometimes weapons for resistance.

Working with a network of friends, Simaite created the Committee to Rescue Jews. The group brought Jewish children out of the ghetto and took them to homes where non-Jews had agreed to hide them. Simaite also removed rare books and documents that were prized by the Jewish people, including drawings, diaries, and other material depicting life in the ghetto. These she hid in special vaults at the university.

In 1942 the Germans began to empty the ghetto and deport its residents to death camps in Poland. By then, the Nazis had arrested Gentiles in Vilna who were helping Jews. The secret police suspected that Simaite was involved in this work. Despite

Anna Simaite, the Lithuanian librarian who went into the ghetto on the pretext of retrieving rare books. Instead, she performed multiple rescue efforts, including bringing food to the needy.

the growing peril, she increased her rescue efforts. To avoid arrest, she moved out of her apartment and hid from the Nazis in the homes of sympathetic people. She continued to escort Jews to hiding places, raise funds for the committee's work, and carry messages and food to people in need.

The Nazis finally caught and arrested Anna Simaite in 1944. She was convicted of crimes against the Nazi regime and sentenced to death, but university officials intervened on her behalf and convinced the Germans to reduce her sentence to imprisonment. Simaite was sent first to Dachau, near Munich, Germany. Later, she was imprisoned in a concentration camp in Southern France.

When Allied troops liberated this camp, Simaite was near death. After months in a hospital, her health broken, she remained in Paris, where she lived quietly and worked as a dishwasher. Some of the people she had helped inquired about Simaite and discovered her whereabouts. They offered her money and housing, but she declined and continued working at various jobs, as a laundress and seamstress.

In 1953, Simaite finally agreed to live in Israel with Tania Wachsman. Wachsman had been a child in the ghetto when Simaite helped her to escape and took her to a hiding place where she remained safe during the war. Now a mother of two, Wachsman opened her home to the woman she called, "My dear Mother." When Anna Simaite arrived in Israel, she was greeted with flowers, gifts, receptions, and admiring newspaper articles, tributes to a modest woman

"Let Us Take Care": Finnish Jews Survive

Nazism did not flourish in Finland, the small Scandinavian nation that borders Russia. As the Nazis persecuted Jews in Germany, Finnish leaders and the Finnish press expressed disapproval. However, as World War II began, Germany's then-ally Russia posed a military threat to Finland. Finns allied themselves with Germany rather than risk losing their independence.

By 1942, German troops occupied northern Finland and the Nazis proposed anti-Jewish laws. They demanded that the government turn over Jewish refugees living in Finland. Officials arranged to transport Jewish refugees to neutral Sweden.

Hitler was bent on deporting the two thousand Finnish Jews who remained. Heinrich Himmler, the head of all Nazi police units, went to Finland to expedite this plan. Accompanying Himmler was his personal physician, Felix Kersten, a native of Estonia who had once served with the Finnish Independence Army. Kersten volunteered to act as an intermediary and was able to warn Finnish leaders about the Nazis' intentions. He also advised Himmler that the Finns opposed attacks on Jews and should not be pushed too quickly.

As talks went on, Finnish intelligence agents confirmed their hunch that the Nazis planned to kill the Jews they deported. Citizens resented Himmler's presence. An editorial in a respected Finnish newspaper described the tragic situation of the Jews. The author warned about the future consequences of aiding the Nazis, saying, "Let us take care . . . that with the return of peace, no shadow is cast across Finland."

Finnish leaders looked for ways to protect Jews. Secretly, they offered the use of ships to Jewish leaders in Helsinki, the capital, if escape became necessary. Meanwhile, Kersten helped the Finns stall for time. By late 1943, a few Jews had been arrested in Finland but no deportations had occurred. Preoccupied with problems elsewhere, German leaders chose not to fight the Finns on this matter.

who had risked her life numerous times to save others.

"You Were Our Last Hope": The Zahajkewycz Family

Orest and Helena Zahajkewycz were sixteen and twenty years old, respectively, in 1941. Their Greek Orthodox family lived in Peremyshl, a Ukrainian city with a population of about fifty thousand. Their father, Bohdan, was a high school literature teacher; their mother, also a teacher, was at the time a homemaker. The family had many Jewish friends. They were especially close to a family named Shefler who had once lived in the same apartment building.

After the Nazi occupation began, Orest was ordered to work in a German military supply factory. Many of his coworkers were Jewish men from the ghetto. Some expressed the hope that if they cooperated and worked hard in the factory, nothing worse would happen to them. But by 1941 they had reason for alarm. As Orest recalls, "Little by little, [the Germans] first took older people in freight trains and shipped them to wherever, no one knew where."[38]

Orest soon guessed what was happening:

Clothing sent for the Germans working in the factory had a hole and a hard spot in it, so I knew people were being shot. Then [a fellow worker] told me he thought they must be killing Jews, and asked if there was any possibility of finding hiding places.[39]

By then a Jewish doctor, Kuba Reinbach, was hiding at the Zahajkewycz home. One night, Helena awoke to the sound of voices in the next room. Her father was talking with a man and woman. The man spoke:

Professor . . . we knocked on every door, and asked them to take me and my wife in to hide for a few days. Everybody closed the door and refused. I didn't want to come to your house [because you have three children] but you were our last hope.[40]

The family sheltered this desperate couple until Orest and Helena could buy them train tickets to Warsaw and safely escort them to that city. From time to time, Orest brought home friends from the factory who were in danger of being sent to Germany for forced labor. They stayed until they could find safe havens, often in the country. Late in the war, the Zahajkewycz family hid Edzo Shefler and his wife in their home for ten months until the war's end. The couple hid in the cellar, then moved into a hiding place the family built in a pantry. The family's situation was all the more precarious

because their home was located across the street from a Ukrainian police station.

Although some of the Jews who hid in their neighborhood were discovered, those sheltered in this home survived the war. In 1985, Orest and Helena were reunited with the Sheflers in Israel when they received their medals from Yad Vashem.

"To Save Somebody's Life Is Not a Shame": Jean Kowalyk

One day in her Ukrainian village, Jean Kowalyk was shocked to see a dear childhood friend, Blumka Friedman, standing behind a barbed wire fence. The Nazis who occupied the town had built a labor camp where Jewish citizens

Along with his family, Orest Zahajkewycz managed to smuggle Jews out of the ghetto and hide them at his home.

"Come Quickly!"

One cold winter night in 1942, six-year-old Debora Biron escaped from the ghetto in Kovno, Lithuania. She and another child walked out of the open gate just as a returning men's work brigade walked in. A Lithuanian Catholic woman standing in the shadows called out to them, "Come quickly!"

The two girls were concealed in a hay wagon and taken to a safe house. A month later, they arrived at the farm of a family named Karashka. They were kind but warned Debora she must not be seen by any strangers. Biron told author Maxine Rosenberg:

> I had to stay indoors and be quiet, which meant no shouting or laughing aloud. . . . When Mrs. Karashka tucked me into bed, she talked softly to me and did whatever she could to make me feel part of her family. But I was still sad.

Debora was thrilled when her mother joined her in hiding. Several other adults also came. By now, Germans were all over the area. The Karashkas built a bunker with a trap door next to their cellar. At night, the adults took turns guarding the trap door while the others slept on the earthen floor. Bombings overhead added to their terror of being discovered.

One night, the people in hiding heard the sound of German boots entering the house. The trap door was open. With great care, one of the men pulled it with a stick until it quietly closed. "Who's down there?" a soldier shouted. "It's only my child and me," Mrs. Karashka called from the cellar under the kitchen.

Even so, the soldier went downstairs. As the people in the bunker waited breathlessly, he looked around, then left. Afterwards, they marveled that they had not been caught. Biron also gained a new respect for the protectors. She recalls:

> Now I could better understand how the Karashkas were protecting us. All along . . . my mother had told me what wonderful people they were, and although I liked them a lot, I didn't realize until that night how they were risking their lives for us.

A month later, the village was liberated and the Germans were forced out. A few days later, Debora and her mother left the farm to begin new lives. After moving to the United States in 1947, they continued to send the Karashka family cards and gifts through the years to show their gratitude.

were forced to live. Kowalyk stared in horror at her friend and the other thin, ragged, frightened people trapped inside the camp. Impulsively, she took a sandwich from her purse and passed it over the fence. Kowalyk continued to bring food to the camp even after a Gestapo guard shot at her one day.

A physician, Solomon Berger, was planning to escape from the camp and begged Kowalyk to hide him. Within months, Kowalyk and her mother were hiding not only Berger but six other Jews who had managed to leave the camp. Kowalyk's brother built a double wall in the attic that would provide concealment, if needed; the seven people could hide in the space between the walls if they stood close together. He also found safe hiding places for twelve other people from the camp. Sadly, Blumka and all her family except one brother could not escape and later were killed by the Nazis.

Kowalyk was a tiny woman who had suffered a broken spine at age six. Yet she showed great physical endurance and courage during the eighteen months she sheltered the escapees. She and her mother carried out the many tasks required to keep seven people alive and safe. They prepared and carried food, washed and ironed their clothing, brought them water and other things they needed, and carried their waste down from the attic each day. In addition, they tried to bolster their spirits and find ways for them to pass the long, nerve-wracking days in hiding. Downstairs, Kowalyk continued her daily work as a seamstress and sewing teacher, presenting an unchanged face to the neighborhood.

Because they lived on a main street in a town known for strong anti-Semitism, the Kowalyks faced special risks. Nazis searched the house several times but did not find the people in the attic. Jean Kowalyk's sister was also hiding people. Friends who knew their secret urged both of them to send the Jews away so that they themselves would no longer face such mortal danger. Kowalyk's nephew told her, "Auntie, don't listen to them. To save somebody's life is not a shame."[41]

For the Kowalyks—Jean, her mother, her sister, her brother—saving lives was something they felt they must do, despite the grave risks. Thousands of other righteous individuals in this region, many of whose names remain unknown, did the same.

Religious Rescuers

Religious leaders in eastern Europe and the Soviet Union responded in different ways to the Nazis. Some protested, more or less vigorously; others remained silent. Many priests who urged their congregants to oppose the Nazis were arrested and sent to concentration camps. Clergy of various faiths who protested Nazi violence toward Jews often found themselves in the so-called pastors' barracks section of Dachau.

In Vilna, Archbishop Rainis encouraged his congregants to help Jews in need. A number of religious orders responded by hiding Jews from the Nazis. Nuns at the Catholic convent in Vilna hid people who escaped from the ghetto, sometimes disguising them in nuns' habits. The women also worked hard each day to find food for their

A Jewish boy, Janek Karzynski (left of priest) hides among a group of altar boys in Kraków, Poland. Many Catholic clergy hid Jews in convents during the war.

"guests." When mass deportations from the Vilna ghetto to relocation in "the East" were recognized as one-way transports to concentration camps, a number of these nuns volunteered to go along to console and even die with them, so strong were their religious principles.

A Lithuanian priest, Father Jonas of Vidukle, did give his life to defend others. When he saw that the Jews in his city were being forced inside the synagogue and would soon be killed, he hid thirty Jewish children in his church. The Germans heard that the children were inside the church and broke down the door. When they demanded that Father Jonas give up the children, he told the Germans they would have to kill him first. They shot him at once and proceeded to murder the defenseless children.

Thousands of other Righteous Gentiles in Europe were also shot, hanged, stabbed, beaten, or deprived of their health and property in concentration camps after they were caught helping or hiding Jews. The Nazis showed no mercy to those who interfered with their war against the Jewish people.

Righteous Gentiles in Scandinavia and the Low Countries

The Scandinavian countries—Norway, Denmark, and Sweden—and Low Countries—Belgium, the Netherlands, and Luxembourg—declared themselves neutral when World War II began. Regardless, in the spring of 1940, Hitler ordered his troops to invade these small democratic nations in western Europe.

For many Jews, this was the second time they would face Nazi persecution. Tens of thousands of refugees from Germany, Austria, and eastern Europe had fled to these countries during the 1930s. The Lipski family was among them.

"To Offer You What I Can": A Family Survives in Belgium

One night in October 1942, Abram Lipski, a Polish-born Jew who had come to Belgium in 1932, walked furtively along the streets of Ghent. In his arms he carried his three-year-old son, Raphael, called Raffi. For several months, Abram and his wife, Tanya, had sought a hiding place for their son. The couple planned to hide themselves separately, believing that apart their risk of detection was reduced.

Finding a non-Jew willing to take in Raffi had been difficult, but, at last, Abram Lipski found Henriette Chaumat, a single, independent woman. When Lipski asked

her to take the boy, she agreed without hesitation. Now, as he hurried toward her apartment, Lipski found himself wondering:

What kind of people would make a man run through the streets like this with his child so that the child would not be murdered? Did this ever happen to anyone else in the history of the world? Could these men be made of the same flesh and bones as I?[42]

Soon after this night, Abram and Tanya Lipski went to stay with Christian friends. But an informer in the neighborhood forced them to look for another place. They found refuge at a small home shared by two couples, Hermine and Ceril Van Assche and Zulma and Pieter Henry, each of whom had a young child. Hermine had once worked in the Lipski home. Not only did these couples agree the Lipskis could come, they promised they could stay as long as necessary. Pieter Henry, Hermine's brother-in-law, said, "For people like you, it gives me pleasure to show my respect and to offer you what I can."[43]

The Lipskis would remain there for two years, while Raffi stayed with Madame Chaumat. For six months after she took him into her city apartment, Chaumat kept Raffi inside; she taught him that his name was now Nicholas and that she was his aunt. When her city neighbors began to seem overly curious about the child, Chaumat moved with Raffi to a small village where she let the local people believe that he was her child, born out of wedlock.

One day, she had a terrible scare when two women came up to the child calling, "Raffi! Raffi!" Chaumat told them, "What are you saying? You've scared my Nick."[44] She hurried home with the child, but for days Chaumat worried that these women, whose brother was a Belgian Fascist, would betray them. Informed of the incident, Abram Lipski decided to send the women a letter, which read in part:

> We know you have discovered our son. His life is in your hands. But don't suppose for a moment that if you give him over to your brother any one of you will go free. I will make you responsible. I hope you have enough heart not to kill an innocent child.[45]

Meanwhile, Raffi's parents adjusted to life in the attic at their hosts' house. The windows in this room were completely blocked to the outside world. But sometimes Lipski left to handle an important matter regarding his business, which was run by a Gentile friend. He needed the income from his business to pay for food and other things the family needed in hiding. Lipski would sneak out on rainy nights, careful to avoid German patrols.

Nazis march through the streets of Denmark during occupation. The Danes resisted Nazi efforts to isolate and deport Jews.

Thanks to their Gentile rescuers, the Lipskis survived. Abram says:

> To [hide Jews] took courage, a pure heart, and a pure motive. In all the time we were hidden Henry and his household never wavered. Sometimes, at night, when we were listening to the BBC [British radio broadcast], I would try to tell him how badly we felt at being such a long-term burden and danger to him and his family. But he would not listen to that.[46]

Pieter Henry took such care to protect the Lipskis that when his brother revealed that he was hiding a Jew in his home, Henry did not reveal that he was doing the same thing. Instead, he asked, "Are you afraid?" No, his brother answered. "If I had a Jew in my house," Henry responded, "I'd be scared."[47]

The brave individuals who sheltered Abram Lipski saved not only his life but his faith in humanity. Other fortunate Jews in Belgium were sustained by ordinary citizens as well as by the strong Belgian resistance movement and by many clergy and nuns.

"Wrap Your Children Up Well": Rescues in Norway

Helen Astrup, a Norwegian, agreed to take part in a daring wartime rescue. Her role required her to claim a coffin, pretending to be a relative of the deceased, and then accompany it on a nighttime drive to Oslo, supposedly for the funeral. However, inside the coffin were two living, very frightened people: her Jewish neighbor Mrs. Hirschfeldt and Mrs. Hirschfeldt's young daughter, Sara. From Oslo, the Hirschfeldts would be taken to safety in neutral Sweden.

Astrup picked up the coffin as she had been instructed and embarked on what turned into a harrowing trip. The car was stopped twice by German officials who examined the vehicle and questioned its occupants. The second time, Germans surrounded the car and ordered everyone out. The coffin was placed on the snowy ground; guards were posted and the other Germans proceeded to drive away in her car.

Left there with the driver and the coffin, Astrup worried that the Hirschfeldts must be bitterly cold. She was terrified that they would move or make a sound of some kind. Worse yet, snow was falling all around. The warmth of the two bodies inside the coffin melted snow that settled on its lid—a sure sign that living people were inside. Thinking quickly, Astrup told the Germans she felt ill, and she sat down on the coffin.

For an hour, she struggled to act normal by chatting amiably with the guards. The men became friendly—too friendly—and began making sexual remarks. As Astrup grew increasingly uncomfortable, the car returned: The Germans had just wanted to borrow it. They allowed Astrup and her driver (who did not know about the Hirschfeldts) to take the coffin and be on their way. The Hirschfeldts reached Sweden safely.

A Jewish Norwegian, Mrs. Henriette Samuel was alerted to danger by a telephone call one evening in late November 1942. A female voice on the other end advised her, "The night is very cold. I suggest that you wrap your children up well."[48] Samuel guessed what this woman, a member of the Norwegian resistance, was trying to tell her in this cryptic message. She proceeded to awaken her three children and hurriedly dress them. Two months earlier her husband, Julius Samuel, the chief rabbi of Norway, had been arrested. She had not heard from him since.

Soon the caller, Inge Sletten Fostyedt, arrived to escort the family, as well as Mrs. Samuel's sister-in-law and her two children, to private homes where they would be safe. In December, they joined other Jews on a risky trip to Sweden. Covered with tarpaulins, they were loaded onto trucks that were supposedly carrying potatoes. Fostyedt later helped Mrs. Samuel's brother-in-law, and she rescued fourteen Jewish Viennese refugees whom she had cared for in a children's home in Oslo.

Brave Norwegians like Inge Fostyedt managed to save about 930 people by smuggling them across the border. The Swedish government actively aided these rescue efforts by giving refuge to Jews who reached their country. They also offered citizenship to Jews with any ties to Sweden.

Against the Odds: Dutch Rescuers

During the early 1930s, about twenty-five thousand German Jews fled to Holland. Later, thousands more refugees—Austrians, Czechs, Poles, and others—joined them. Dutch laws had granted religious freedom in the 1600s, and violence against Jews had not occurred here as it had in eastern Europe. Dutch Jews were well assimilated in a society known for religious tolerance. There was a Dutch Nazi Party, but anti-

Semitism was neither deeply rooted nor widespread. Most citizens opposed Nazism.

Yet about 80 percent of the 140,000 Jews in Holland died during the Holocaust. Why did so many perish in a land known for tolerance and just laws? For one thing, the Nazis set up a brutal occupation government in Holland. A zealous Austrian Nazi, Arthur Seyss-Inquart, was appointed Reichskommissar, or chief administrator, reporting directly to Hitler and Heinrich Himmler, Gestapo chief and head of the Nazi extermination campaign. The Nazis told Dutch officials and Jewish leaders that their cooperation would mean fewer actions against Jews—a blatant lie. Second, Dutch

These Jews escaped from other European nations to find refuge in neutral Sweden.

Nazis were willing informants and helped the Germans to round up Jews for deportation. After the war, many of these collaborators were arrested; more than fifty thousand Dutch people were convicted of treason.

Third, Holland offered few natural hiding places or escape routes. Jews were trapped in a small, flat, open country whose borders and neighbors were under Nazi control. German boats in the North Sea cut off a route to England. To reach neutral Spain or Switzerland, refugees had to cross occupied France. Within Holland itself, German troops controlled the canals, railroads, and bridges.

But the Christian churches continued to speak out against Nazism and the persecution of Jews. Leaders of the Dutch Reformed Church wrote frequent letters to Nazi officials, opposing various policies. Some churches banned their members from joining the Nazi Party. Few of the twelve thousand Dutch Gentiles married to Jews followed Nazi urging to divorce their spouses. Thousands of Dutch people rescued Jews, either on their own or as part of an organized resistance group.

"Dark and Terrible Times": Hidden in Amsterdam

Miep Gies and her husband, Jan, are two of the best-known Dutch rescuers, in connection with the famous diary kept by the young Jewish girl Anne Frank. Gies first

Jews hide in Amsterdam. Anne Frank and her family also found refuge with a family in Amsterdam.

Murdered Hero: Joop Westerweel

Joop Westerweel led a group of Dutch rescuers who helped 150 to 200 Jews escape occupied Holland. Westerweel was a school principal when the war broke out. After anti-Jewish laws were passed, he began renting apartments in his own name so that Jewish families could live there with less fear of being discovered.

In 1942, Jewish students from the group Aliyat Ha-Noar (Youth Aliyah) asked Westerweel to help children escape from Holland. He agreed at once, later explaining, "I felt I had reached a dead end. When one tries to teach in the face of this humiliation to humanity, it is impossible."

Through his network, Jews were smuggled out of Belgium and France through the mountains into Switzerland or Spain. Westerweel himself guided several groups to safety. His wife, Wilhelmina (Will), was also actively involved. In March 1944, the forty-five-year-old Westerweel was captured by Nazis during one of his missions to France. Despite five months of repeated torture, he refused to name anyone else in the rescue group. Joop was executed on August 11. His wife spent fifteen months in a concentration camp but survived.

Before he died, Westerweel wrote letters urging others to continue helping those in need. Promising not to betray anyone, he said, "If we do not meet again, I hope what we did together will remain a sacred memory for life." Sophie Nussbaum, one of the Jews he saved, later said, "I'll never forget him. In those dark days, he was the only spark of humanity."

Joop Westerweel, Dutch Christian Socialist, teacher, and Righteous Gentile.

met German businessman Otto Frank in 1933 when he hired her to work at the food-products business he had started in Amsterdam. The two families became friends through the 1930s and into the Dutch occupation.

By 1942 Frank had already made plans to take his wife and two daughters into hiding, and Gies had agreed to help. That July sixteen-year-old Margot Frank, Anne's older sister, received a letter ordering her to report for deportation to a labor camp in

Germany. On a rainy Monday morning, Miep Gies bicycled to the Franks' home to pick up Margot. She took her to the hiding place, located in a secret annex of the building containing Frank's business offices and warehouse. Had the two women been caught, both would have been arrested. The other three Franks arrived later that same day. Gies and some of her coworkers continued to keep the business running as they cared for the people in hiding.

Miep and Jan Gies were asked to help others as well. Late one night, a woman brought two small children to their apartment, stranded by their parents' arrest. The Gieses cared for the children until they were taken to a safe home. Miep Gies recalls, "Discreet inquiries were made. We discovered an organization of students in Amsterdam that had addresses where children could be brought."[49] Many children were hidden on farms in rural Holland, especially the northern province of Friesland. Later, the Gieses hid a young Dutchman who was being sought by the Nazis.

Meanwhile, a family of three and a dentist joined the Franks in hiding. By now, roundups—*razias*—of Jews were occurring

Miep and Jan Gies hid Anne Frank and other Jews in an attic that Anne dubbed "The Secret Annex." Miep Gies is haunted by memories of the Franks' capture by Nazis: "Never a day goes by that I do not think of what happened then."

"It's Wrong Here"

On Friday, August 4, 1944, disaster struck at the office building in Amsterdam where the Franks and their friends were hiding. Miep Gies was seated at her desk when a policeman arrived. "Don't move," he told her, pointing a gun. Three other employees who were helping the Franks were also at work that day; one man was taken into an office for questioning.

At once, Gies reached into her desk, grabbed the illegal ration cards, money, and other incriminating things that she kept there, and placed them in a bag. She knew her husband, Jan, would soon arrive to meet her for lunch. Before he could step inside, she handed him the bag, saying, "It's wrong here." He left immediately.

With a sinking heart, Gies waited to be interrogated. A policeman screamed at her as he examined her identity papers and located the keys that would unlock the hiding place. As the Nazis went up to the annex to arrest her friends, Gies was in shock: "I felt as if I was falling into a bottomless hole."

After the Nazis left, Gies and two coworkers went upstairs. Their friends were gone. Scattered on the floor were their belongings, including Anne's diary and other writings. After Gies retrieved them, she hid them in her desk—"until she comes back," she said hopefully. Gies later bravely approached Nazi officials and offered to ransom the Franks, but to no avail.

Tragically, Anne Frank did not come back. Anne, Margot, and their mother perished of illness in concentration camps just weeks before the war ended. Otto Frank alone returned to Amsterdam, where he lived for a while with Miep and Jan Gies. Miep was able to give Otto Frank his daughter's diary, which he edited and published. This poignant work by a teenager whose vibrant life was tragically cut short has become known throughout the world.

regularly. Gies and the other helpers worked hard to keep the annex inhabitants safe, healthy, and fed. In Germany and occupied countries, people needed ration cards in order to buy food and other goods legally. Those who were hiding could no longer obtain these cards. The Dutch underground provided stolen or forged cards for rescuers who then used these tickets to buy extra food. To avoid suspicion, Gies made modest purchases on numerous trips to different shops. One grocer noticed how much she was buying: Without saying a word, he began setting aside extra vegetables, which he brought out from another part of the store when Gies came in.

Like many rescuers, Gies strove to help those in hiding live as well as possible under the circumstances. She brought books and magazines, shared news, offered comfort and moral support, and planned special occasions such as birthday parties. Every weekday morning she visited the annex and asked her friends what they needed. Another employee, Elli Vossen, visited at lunch. In the afternoon, Miep's husband went up;

Miep returned in the late afternoon with food and other parcels and spent time visiting. Gies also enrolled in correspondence courses so that Anne and Margot could study stenography during the long months of inactivity.

Their fears rose in 1944. Gies recalls, "Daily, people in hiding were being captured. There were raids and betrayals. The price for turning in a Jew or any person in hiding was going up all the time."[50] One spring night, thieves broke into the warehouse. The Franks worried that they might have been heard moving about.

Around that time, Gies heard distressing news at the shop whose kind owner sold her extra vegetables. When she went in one day, the man's wife came out to wait on her. She said sadly, "My husband's been arrested. . . . He was hiding Jews. Two Jews. I don't know what they'll do to him."[51]

Within months, Gies herself would endure a Nazi raid and see her dear friends arrested. In a memoir written many years after the diary of the child she sheltered had become known around the world, she wrote:

I am not a hero. I stand at the end of the long, long line of good Dutch people who did what I did or more—much more—during those dark and terrible times years ago but always like yesterday in the hearts of those of us who bear witness. Never a day goes by that I do not think of what happened then.[52]

Aart and Johtje Vos

Aart and Johtje Vos managed to hide more than three dozen people in their home in Laren, outside Amsterdam, in addition to caring for their four young children. All survived, thanks to the kind and resourceful Voses. Their rescue work began, as Johtje recalls, when they agreed to safeguard a suitcase for a Jewish friend: "And then a week later, somebody would ask you, 'Well, my child is in danger.' So we said, 'Of course, bring him here.' Then two people said, 'Well, we don't know where to go.'"[53]

Within months, they became deeply involved in a rescue network and more and more people sought refuge at their home. The Voses were lucky to live near a wooded area on a dead-end road. Beneath a coal bin with a false bottom, they built a tunnel that led from their shed under the garden and into the woods. At times, members of the resistance would warn the Voses that Nazis were searching homes; then, their "guests" would enter the tunnel.

The Voses had several narrow escapes during the five years of Nazi occupation. During one raid, as soldiers searched nearby, a man they were hiding became distraught and had to be restrained from leaping to his death from a window. Another time, police came to the house searching

Aart and Johtje Vos hid as many as thirty-six Jewish friends and strangers in their home.

The Gentiles who hid or helped Jews went to great lengths to conceal their activities. Often, they told nobody, not even close friends or family members, what they were doing. Many were constantly on guard. They had to avoid being seen when they brought extra groceries or supplies home. They took care not to put out too much garbage or to hang extra garments on outdoor clotheslines. Children in the family, unable to invite others to visit, were not spared constraints. Aart Vos says in *Rescuers: Portraits of Moral Courage in the Holocaust*:

> The biggest enemy was people talking. I went to visit in the home of van Gogh's nephew one day, and he gave me an envelope. I asked, "What's in it?" He told me, "It's money for the work you're doing."
>
> Vos told him that he must have "the wrong Vos" and refused the money.
>
> Recalling this experience, Vos comments, "You just couldn't trust anyone."

As she prepared to face the Gestapo, Johtje knew that the lives of dozens of people rested on her actions during the next few minutes. Quickly, she grabbed the incriminating papers. Seeing no good hiding place, she stuffed them into her son's sweater and told him to leave the room as quickly and quietly as possible. Johtje then managed to convince the Gestapo that she did not have the stamp in her possession. Later, she felt awful about the risk her son had endured on that day. Her mother had told Johtje she did not have the right to endanger her children. Johtje recalls:

> My husband and I talked to her, and said, "We find it more important for our children to have parents who have done what they felt they had to do—even if it costs their lives. It will be better for them—even if we don't make it. They will know we did what we felt we had to do." My mother fully understood this and agreed.[54]

The Voses and the people they hid lived to celebrate the liberation of Holland in May 1945. Aart and Johtje have said that their strong, loving relationship and their belief that they were doing the right thing saw them through.

A Nation of Righteous Citizens: Denmark

Denmark has been honored as a nation of Righteous Gentiles by Yad Vashem. Nearly all the Jews who lived in Denmark as of 1940 survived the war, even though Nazis occupied the country for five years. Danes expressed disbelief and disgust when the Germans arrived in April 1940 and began persecuting Jews. They were able to influence some of the German soldiers stationed

for a stamp that was used to forge illegal documents. A man in their rescue group had been arrested, and the Voses had in their possession both the stamp and a pile of incriminating documents. Seeing the police, Aart Vos led the group of Jews through the tunnel into the woods.

in Denmark, and some of these Germans began helping the Danish resistance.

Nazi officials had decreed that all Jews over age six in occupied countries must wear a yellow cloth Star of David. A story circulated that King Christian X and his family announced they would wear the star themselves "as a badge of honor." The king said, "The Jews are a part of the Danish nation. We have no Jewish problem in our country because we never had an inferiority complex in relation to the Jews."[55]

The Danish Freedom Council issued a proclamation that condemned anti-Jewish measures. It said, in part:

We Danes know that the whole population stands behind resistance to the German oppressors. The Council calls on the Danish population to help in every way possible those Jewish fellow-citizens who have not yet succeeded in escaping abroad. Every Dane who renders help to the Germans in their persecution of

Aart and Johtje Vos point to Allied planes during liberation. With them are their own children and members of two Jewish families the Voses helped hide.

human beings is a traitor and will be punished as such when Germany is defeated.[56]

In 1943 the Danes learned of German plans to deport Danish Jews. Georg Ferdinand Duckwitz, a German naval attaché stationed in Denmark, heard that a roundup was scheduled on September 28; he proceeded to warn his Danish friends.

The word spread. A young woman named Inge Barfeldt told Rabbi Marcus Melchior, who then warned his Copenhagen congregation that they must all be in hiding by the next night. An ambulance driver in Copenhagen scanned the telephone book for people whose names sounded Jewish. He then drove around the city, warning people.

People hid Jews in their homes. Sympathetic doctors admitted Jews to hospitals under false names. One Copenhagen hospital ran fake funeral services in its chapel. Dressed in black, Jews hid there until they could leave safely.

The Danes then transported thousands of Jews across the sea to neutral Sweden. Former Danish ambassador to the United Nations Leif Donde was seven years old when he was rescued. He recalls the dramatic eleven-hour journey with sixteen other refugees on board:

> The boat was handled by a couple of young men, nineteen and twenty-one years old, who had no previous experience running a boat. One hour out to sea, German patrol boats detected us and started to give chase. . . . The weather turned rough—we were awfully sick—and twice the engine failed.[57]

Despite these problems, the boat reached a Swedish harbor two hours before sinking.

Rabbi Marcus Melchior warned members of his Copenhagen synagogue that the Germans intended to round up Denmark's Jews.

One very active Danish rescuer was Ellen Nielsen, a widowed mother of six who sold fish for a living. Nielsen hid more than one hundred people in her home as they waited their turn on the boats. She continued to resist the Nazis and was arrested in December 1944, charged with having helped Jews leave Denmark. Nielsen spent several months in German concentration camps. Three times she was put in lines en route to the gas chambers. Each time she eluded death, either by slipping out of line or because the guards ordered her group back to its barracks. Nielsen survived the war.

Danes in Elsinore, located a few miles opposite Sweden, also played a major role in the rescue effort. Dr. Jorgens Gersfelt gave

Righteous Gentiles in Scandinavia and the Low Countries   55

children sedatives to keep them quiet on the boats and used his extra gas rations to drive Jews to the docks. Bookbinder Erlin Kiaer made numerous trips to Sweden and back, piloting fishing boats that contained refugees. The Nazis found out about Kiaer's activities and set out to find him. After his arrest, Kiaer was tortured during a long interrogation, but he betrayed no one.

Nearly eight thousand people—98.5 percent of all Danish Jews and Jewish refugees from other lands—reached Sweden safely. Historians have speculated that the German occupation forces under General Werner Best may have spotted some of the rescue boats but decided not to interfere. Raul Hilberg, a leading Holocaust scholar, points out that German power was limited in the face of such unified resistance; even Danish police would not arrest Jews. Many agree with author Robert Goldston, who says, "There could be little doubt that where a conquered people was prepared to resist the 'final solution to the Jewish problem,' that 'solution' could not be carried out."[58]

5 Righteous Gentiles in France

France collapsed in June 1940 after a swift and forceful German invasion. Germany annexed Alsace-Lorraine and divided France into two parts. The north was occupied by the Nazis; the south was designated a Free Zone, under the aging military leader Marshal Philippe Pétain and a puppet government at Vichy. (By late 1942, the Nazis would also occupy southern France.)

The right-leaning Vichy government collaborated with the Nazis in various ways during the occupation. Vichy passed anti-Jewish laws on its own and rounded up people to be deported. Xavier Vallat, a virulent anti-Semite, was appointed to head the Commission on Jewish Affairs. But though a number of anti-Semitic French aided the Nazis, others worked hard to resist.

When the war began, about 1 percent of the French population was Jewish, some 350,000 people, half of whom had long-standing roots in France. The others were refugees who had come from other countries. About 75 percent survived the war. At first, the government took some measures to protect French-born Jews; only about 14 percent of these native French Jews perished compared with nearly 30 percent of the 175,000 Jewish refugees who were living in France.

Some Jews survived because it was easier to escape from France than from some other countries. France had many ports and bordered two neutral countries, Spain and Switzerland, as well as Italy, a country that resisted anti-Jewish actions. About thirty

German troops parade down the Champs-Élysées after the fall of Paris in 1940. The Vichy government readily collaborated with the Nazis.

thousand Jews who fled from central Europe went first to France, then to Spain, from which they escaped to the United States. Others reached Africa, Palestine, Italy, and Switzerland. A Jewish assistance program called HICEM helped refugees, but was hindered by red tape, the problems of obtaining exit visas, and a lack of funds and transportation. Yet a higher percentage of Jews were smuggled out of France to safety than in other countries.

Thousands of Jews also went into hiding in France during the occupation. The majority sought refuge in 1942, when the Nazis began mass deportations to the Polish death camps. The Nazis planned a massive roundup in Paris for July 16, but some French police and officials heard about it and warned Jews and members of the resistance. Even so, the Nazis arrested about eleven thousand people, including four thousand children.

Many French people who witnessed the raids and deportations expressed disgust. Those brave enough to help Jews had to contend with both the Nazis and French collaborators, including two fascist paramilitary groups, the Milice (militia) and the SEC (Sections d'Enquete et Controle). However, Nazis complained that local law enforcement inadequately enforced anti-Jewish measures and sometimes helped Jews. And a pro-Nazi journalist named Jacques Marcy complained, "Every Catholic family shelters a Jew." [59]

Had Marcy's words been true, more Jews would have survived. However, in one remarkable mountain community, five thousand people devoted themselves to saving at least that many lives.

"The Word of the Lord"

Inspired by an energetic team of strong-minded Protestant ministers and their compassionate, hardworking wives, the villagers of Le Chambon and surrounding villages in south-central France defied the Nazis. André and Magda Trocmé had come to Le Chambon from the mining area of northern France, where Trocmé had ministered to laborers and the poor. He believed in nonviolence and was deeply committed to the international peace movement. With fellow minister Edouard Theis, Trocmé founded the Cevenol School in Le Chambon. There, young people prepared for university study and learned pacifist principles of tolerance, nonviolence, and justice.

A propaganda poster enjoins passersby to become part of the Milice, France's political police. French citizens were divided over the Nazis' deportation of Jews.

"I Cannot but Act": Aristides de Sousa Mendes

In 1940 nearly one hundred thousand Jews lived in the city of Bordeaux, France. As the Nazis poured into the country, thousands of people hoped to cross the Pyrenees into Spain by way of neutral Portugal.

Aristides de Sousa Mendes, the Portuguese ambassador to France, had been ordered to cease issuing visas to Jewish refugees, but his conscience told him otherwise. Seeing the desperate people who lined up outside his door, he continued to write visas, and he also let people stay in his home. With his family's help, Mendes kept stamping visas for three days. By this time, the Germans had taken over France, and Mendes's government notified him to return at once to Portugal.

As he was leaving the country, Mendes found other ways to aid refugees. He stamped visas in the town of Bayonne, where he outranked the other Portuguese officials, then helped groups of refugees find the best border stations to pass through.

In the end, Mendes helped about thirty thousand refugees, but he paid a high price. The Portuguese Foreign Ministry was upset that he had disobeyed their orders not to give visas to the thousands of refugees who now entered the country. This father of twelve children lost his license to practice law and was removed from the diplomatic corps, his pension denied. Before he died in poverty in 1954, Mendes had explained his actions in France, saying, "I cannot but act as a Christian." He has said that he would do the same thing again under the same conditions and declared, "I accept everything that has befallen me with love."

Years after his death, Mendes was honored as a hero. In 1966, Yad Vashem issued a commemorative medal in his name. The Portuguese government awarded him the Order of Freedom in 1987. The next year, his position in the Foreign Ministry was restored. The national assembly agreed that his back pay and pension should be restored to Mendes's descendants.

Trocmé had been impressed with the faith and commitment of the villagers when he arrived at Le Chambon. He said, "These people . . . do not stand on the moving soil of opinion but on the rock of the Word of the Lord."[60] Magda Trocmé believed that many people in the area were prepared to help others because of their history: "Their ancestors were the old Huguenots [or Protestants] who . . . were persecuted by the Catholic kings of France. They often talked about their ancestors. . . . When the Germans came, they remembered and were able to understand the persecution of the Jews."[61]

Magda Trocmé was working in her kitchen one freezing winter day in 1941 when a woman, trembling with cold and fear, knocked on her door. As Magda recalled, the woman "said immediately that she was a German Jew, that she was running away, that she was hiding, that she wanted to have shelter. She thought that at a minister's house she would perhaps find someone who could understand her. And I said, 'Come in.'"[62] Magda offered the woman warmth, dry clothing, and food.

The need to help refugees, most of whom were Jews, was clear to the Trocmés. When André asked leaders of the American Friends Service Committee (a Quaker organization) how he could help, they suggested that Trocmé's area could shelter refugees, especially children. Trocmé then discussed the plan with his church council and they agreed. Refugees were placed in more than twelve boardinghouses and several group homes sponsored by various organizations—the World Council of Churches; Swiss Help to Children; the CIMADE (Comite d'Inter-Mouvements Aupres des Evacues), a Protestant women's group; and the OSE (Oevre de Secours aux Enfants) a Jewish child-care organization, among others. Trocmé and the Quakers believed that besides saving lives, they must help to restore these children's faith in humankind.

As more and more people took part in rescue work, some of them also taking refugees into their homes. The area's Protestant ministers inspired them with sermons about how to overcome evil with goodness.

One summer day in 1942, a prominent police official came to Le Chambon and confronted Trocmé, saying, "You are hiding in this commune a certain number of Jews, whose names I know."[63] He ordered Trocmé to give him a list of these people and their addresses or face arrest and deportation. Magda Trocmé recalls that André refused: "My husband said, 'No I cannot. First, I do not know their names'—they often changed their names—'and I don't know who they are. And second, these Jews, they are my brothers.'"[64]

One French official persisted, telling Trocmé that Jews were neither his brothers nor from his country nor of his religion. Magda remembers that her husband told the men they were wrong, saying, "Here, they are under my protection."[65]

The police left, but Trocmé feared that there would be one more raid coming in the area. Local Boy Scouts and a wide network of people immediately warned the refugees in the area and on surrounding farms that Jews should hide in the woods for a day or two. On Sundays, ministers delivered ringing sermons in the crowded churches. They exhorted people to obey God, not man, when the government broke God's commandments. They

The Trocmé family in Le Chambon: (back row) André and Magda; (front row) Daniel, Jacques, Jean-Pierre, Nelly. The Trocmés led the rescue effort of Jews in Le Chambon.

quoted passages from the Old Testament warning people to give refuge to those in need "lest innocent blood be shed in your land."[66]

Trocmé and Theis were arrested by the French police, along with Roger Darcissac, head of the village public school. They spent four weeks in an internment camp in the southwest of France, near Limoges, but were released.

The Nazis planned to capture Trocmé and Theis in 1943. An anonymous warning came that the Gestapo intended to assassinate them. Trocmé reluctantly agreed to hide in the mountains during the last year of the war. He was forced to move from place to place as the Gestapo tried to track him down. While living at a home in Drôme, Trocmé's son Jacques was able to join him for a few months, a happy experience for them both. Trocmé continued to suffer the threat of discovery as well as chronic pain due to a ruptured disc in his spine.

Meanwhile, Edouard Theis, who was physically stronger, joined an underground organization that helped Jews escape to Switzerland. His missions were especially risky, since the Gestapo had put him on their death list, too. The inhabitants of the area continued their work until they were liberated in the summer of 1944. On June 6, as the Allies landed on the beaches at Normandy, André and Jacques Trocmé returned home at last.

The residents of the area accepted the challenge during the Holocaust. Looking back on those days, Magda Trocmé, who was also rearing four young children and teaching at the Cevenol School during the war, says, "Each person, each day, did what seemed necessary."[67] No person was ever turned away; no Jew or rescuer was betrayed. The actions of these people reflected the essential teaching of Christianity: Love thy

A Filmmaker's Tribute: Pierre Sauvage

Filmmaker Pierre Sauvage was born in March 1944 in occupied France. He recalls, "It was in Le Chambon that I was born . . . lucky to see the light of day in a place on earth singularly committed to my survival at a time when much of my family was disappearing into the abyss."

Sauvage later moved to the United States and settled in California. He formed a group called The Friends of Le Chambon and became its first president. During the 1980s, Sauvage returned to Le Chambon in order to make a documentary about this remarkable place. His interviews with villagers who lived there during the war and some of the people they sheltered are featured in his acclaimed film, "Weapons of the Spirit." In the film's narration, Sauvage gives the historical context of the war while describing the rescue work and the people who made it possible.

Summarizing what happened at Le Chambon, Sauvage says, "When their hearts spoke to them, they first listened, then they acted." He has continued to speak about his experiences so that people will know about the courageous goodness shown by these villagers and their leaders during the Holocaust.

This group portrait shows Jewish children in front of La Guespy children's home in Le Chambon. The rescue effort at Le Chambon remains remarkable because every citizen in the town made it his or her duty to aid the Jews.

neighbor as thyself. Rescuer Marie Brottes told filmmaker Pierre Sauvage, "The neighbor to love as yourself is down the street."[68]

Righteous Clergy

Other clergy, both Catholic and Protestant, helped Jews. Protestant leaders formed the CIMADE, composed primarily of women. Members of CIMADE did relief work, spoke out against the concentration camps, found safe houses for Jews, and smuggled people across the Swiss border.

In October 1941, the Nazis set out to destroy the synagogues of France. Cardinal Gerlier, the archbishop of Lyons and Catholic leader of France, expressed condolences and concern in a letter to Rabbi Kaplan. The defiant cardinal instructed French Catholics to help Jews in various ways.

Taking action, Cardinal Gerlier sponsored Amities Chretiennes (Christian Friendship), an organization in which both Catholics and Protestants worked to help Jews in hiding. Directed by Father Pierre Chaillet, the group rescued many people. Chaillet published an important underground newspaper and hid Jewish children who had been orphaned or left behind when their parents were arrested or deported. Many were placed in monasteries or in the countryside with peasant families. After the Nazis imprisoned Chaillet in September 1942, other Jesuits continued his work.

That same year, Rabbi Kaplan met with Cardinal Gerlier in Lyons to describe the Nazi brutality he had seen during roundups. Gerlier then met with Protestant pastor Marc Boegner, the cosponsor of Amities Chretiennes, and they decided to protest publicly through letters to the Vichy government.

Some Catholic leaders in the northern zone had protested to government officials when roundups began in Paris. In August 1942, when such "actions" occurred in the south, the archbishop of Toulouse, Monsignor Jules Gerard Saliege (later a cardinal), issued an episcopal protest against the deportation of Jews. As a result, on August 23, every Catholic priest in the diocese of Toulouse read the archbishop's letter from his pulpit. Saliege decried the "dreadful spectacle of men, women, and children being treated like vile beasts; of families being torn apart and deported to unknown destinations."[69] He said that Christianity imposed moral rights and duties that must not be violated.

The archbishop urged Catholics and religious institutions to help the suffering Jews, and many of them accepted the risk. Thousands of people found refuge or escaped to safety with the help of families in this region.

Public outcry continued. Gerlier and Saliege wrote joint letters of protest. As more roundups occurred, clergy of various denominations risked deportation and death to save Jews. They placed children with falsified identify papers in convents, homes, and other safe places. Nuns who ran orphanages and boarding schools frequently hid Jewish children from the Gestapo and French police. Adults were also harbored in such places, sometimes assuming roles as servants, cooks, or gardeners.

"They Were Risking Their Lives": The Fedou and Valat Families

The Kapp family was aided both by concerned individuals and religious institutions in southern France. Late in 1942 the family found themselves on the run, struggling to avoid police roundups. A Gentile named Bernard found the family an apartment above a tobacco shop in the village of Arthes. In the apartment above lived their protectors, a Catholic family named Fedou. Ruth Kapp Hartz, who was five years old at the time, recalls:

A forged passport. During the war, many French clergy illegally obtained such documents for the Jews in their care.

We knew they were risking their lives in order to give us shelter. It was common knowledge by that time that any citizen who was caught harboring Jews would be arrested on the spot and sent, along with the Jews, to a concentration camp. . . . My parents learned, long after our arrival there, that almost every young man in the village was a member of a Resistance group or was able to help the Resistance fighters in some way.[70]

Weeks after their arrival, the Kapps were told about a man who could provide them with false papers and new names. Ruth was instructed to give her name as "Renee," and the family used the last name "Caper." One day, a Protestant clergyman accompanied Mr. Kapp, now Bernard Caper, to Toulouse, in search of news of the fate of some missing relatives.

An older couple named Jeanne and Henri Valat also befriended the Kapps and let them hide in their cellar during especially dangerous times. When they had ample warning of roundups, the family hid in the fields. Ruth says, "The longer we stayed in Arthes, the more people we met, people who were charitable, kind, and trustworthy. These were people who were willing to risk their own lives and safety for us. And they became our friends."[71]

Despite these kindnesses, these were terrifying years for children like Ruth. As she sat in school during the day, she would wonder, "What if Papa and Maman are not there when I get back?"[72] In November 1942 the Kapp family heard over the radio that Nazi troops were heading for southern France, breaking an agreement not to occupy the so-called Free Zone. Now no place in France was safe for Jews. Ruth was to spend some time in a convent before returning to the village, where she

and her family managed to stay alive until France was liberated by the Allies.

Delivered from Death: Raoul Laporterie

Raoul Laporterie, mayor of a village called Grenade-sur-l'Adour, also owned a clothing store in the nearby town of Mont-de-Marsan, so situated that he lived in the free—unoccupied—part of France yet worked in the occupied zone. Laporterie made use of this arrangement to save Jews and other fugitives during the war.

Using the special pass that allowed him to cross the line between the two sections of France, he became a *passeur*. First he took messages and parcels from one zone to the other; in 1941, he began transporting people in his car from the Nazi-occupied north to the south, where their chances of survival were greater. Some *passeurs* charged a fee, but Laporterie helped people for nothing.

Carefully, creatively, he devised methods for moving his passengers safely across the Nazi-guarded border. He gave them false identity papers, then instructed them how to act when guards approached the car or asked questions. People could not take much money, luggage, or belongings without arousing suspicion, so Laporterie stored their possessions in his store until he could return them safely. He also cultivated friendly relations with the guards and learned their habits and schedules. He recalls:

I had my tricks. If passengers were in the car, for example, I always arrived at the frontier at exactly seven-fifty in the evening, ten minutes before the [guards] were to be relieved. They didn't want to waste too much time with us. They wanted their dinner. Besides, I kept them more interested in what I had in

Behind Convent Walls

For several months during 1943, Ruth Kapp lived in a convent at Soreze that operated an orphanage. The Germans knew that some convents hid Jewish children, so raids were common. One day, Ruth was in the infirmary receiving first aid for a cut knee. The nun there, Madame Luis, suddenly looked out the window and exclaimed, "Oh, mon Dieu [my God]! Nazis!" She told Ruth and another girl to hurry back to their classrooms. Kapp recalls in *Your Name Is Renee: Ruth's Story as a Hidden Child*:

> As we reached the last steps, we heard male voices—German—issuing from the room on the right, which I was now certain was the Mother Superior's office. Perhaps the Nazis have come for Emmy, Jean-Claude, and me, I thought. Now everyone will know that I am Jewish. Should I try to run away?

> Both girls stood silent, listening. Kapp

heard an officer say, "Several convents have already been bombed. Of course, you realize the same fate could be yours."

Mother Superior replied, "We have no Jewish children in this convent. This is an orphanage for French children whose parents have been killed in the war. We are quite out of the way, as you see. I cannot imagine how any Jewish refugees would find us." Although the officer persisted, the Mother Superior assured him that the church would not risk the lives of orphans and nuns by sending Jewish children to the convent. She added, "To tell you the truth, we can hardly manage with the number of children we have, what with the food and clothing shortages."

The Nazis left but returned on other occasions. Kapp and the other Jewish children were taken to a secret room in the convent. She remained in the convent for five months before returning to her parents' hiding place in Arthes.

my shop waiting for them than in my passengers. I spoiled them a little.[73]

In 1946, Laporterie was honored for his wartime heroism at a large banquet held in his hometown. Many of the people he helped contacted Laporterie after the war. In one letter, a Mr. Schinazi wrote, "Without this generous help from you—as pure in motive as it was bold—we would have remained in Bordeaux at the mercy of those ferocious beasts who were the Germans and their ignoble collaborators."[74] From

Jerusalem, Isaac Levy wrote, "This heroic gesture on your part we have not forgotten and will never forget."[75]

When Laporterie was honored by Yad Vashem in 1976, he said that during the Holocaust he was moved to help Jews "pass through the holes of the net that was set for them and to find them refuges which put them out of the reaches of the Germans."[76]

"Father of the Jews"

The tireless Pere Marie-Benoit, who belonged to the Capuchin monastic order, aided French Jews and at least twenty-five hundred Italian Jews and fifteen hundred foreign Jews living in Italy during the Holocaust.

The priest who was affectionately called "Father of the Jews" was born in Maine-et-Loire, France, and served in World War I. He became a well-known scholar of Judaism and Hebrew studies. After the Nazi invasion, Pere Marie-Benoit and his fellow monks in Marseilles, France, printed and distributed false documents that would help Jews to conceal their identity and escape. The monks collected money to get refugees to Switzerland and Spain. Their organization gave false ID papers to at least four thousand French Jews.

After the Nazis entered the Free Zone in France, Father Benoit worked with Italian officials to move Jews into the Italian zone, where they would be safer. Angry about this activity, the Nazis told Italian dictator and Axis partner Benito Mussolini to put an end to it. In turn, Mussolini told General Guido Lospinoso to go to Nice and stop Father Marie-Benoit and his group. However, the priest and a prominent Italian Jew, Angelo Donati, met with Lospinoso and won his support. Lospinoso allowed them to continue and even assisted them, making it easier to save more people.

Gisele Warshawsky was among the children who met the priest while she was hiding in an orphanage. She remembers:

Father Benoit used to take some of us younger children out into the field in order to give us an outing. He was very

nice. I was one of the children who was very lucky to be able to go out maybe once a month. We would go to the fields in the rain and try to get berries.[77]

On a visit to Rome, Father Marie-Benoit met with the pope and proposed several new rescue plans. In addition to repatriating Spanish Jews back to safety in Spain, he wanted to move thousands of French Jews to safety in Morocco, Algiers, and Tunisia, now occupied by Allied troops. The Vatican approved these plans, as did the British and U.S. governments. However, German troops reached the Italian zone of the Riviera before the Jews could be moved out; many then fled across the Alps.

By 1943 the Gestapo was determined to capture the defiant priest, so his coworkers urged him to relocate to Rome. There he was known as Father Benedetto. By working with Delasem (Delagazione Assist enza Emigrant Ebitei), a Jewish relief agency that aided refugees, Father Benedetto again began supplying thousands of fake identity and food ration cards needed by people in hiding. These people "became" non-Jewish Swiss, French, Italian, Hungarian, and Romanian citizens.

During the last months of the war, Father Benoit lost several colleagues to Nazi arrest and deportation. The Gestapo arrested and tortured his friend and coworker Brigadier de Marco of the Italian police. But Marie-Benoit/Benedetto continued to fight. After the war, he was honored by the French government and numerous other groups for his rescue activities.

6 Righteous Gentiles in Italy

They called it the "Black Sabbath" raid. Early on the morning of October 16, 1943, Nazi soldiers set out to arrest all the Jews in Rome. German officials had estimated they would seize at least eight thousand people, who would then be crammed into trains bound for camps in Germany and Poland.

When the raid ended nine hours later, the Nazis counted 1,200 captives, including 896 women and children. Among the prisoners were 252 non-Jews, who were released.

Where were the other Jews of Rome? They had found refuge. Some were sheltered by Catholic clergy in monasteries, convents, and in the Vatican complex; others stayed out of sight in private homes, protected by non-Jewish friends and people who hated the Nazis. Next to Denmark, where nearly all Jews escaped from the Nazis, Italian Jews had the highest rates of survival. Of the forty-five thousand Jews who lived there when the war began, thirty-eight thousand were alive at the end. Thousands of refugees from other countries who made their way to Italian-occupied war zones also survived.

How did this relatively high percentage of Jews endure in a country that was allied with Hitler's Germany? Jews in Italy found themselves in peculiar circumstances, facing unique dangers as well as certain advantages. For one thing, the geography of Italy favored escape and difficulty of detection—the country has many ports and some mountainous areas.

Italy also had a tradition of tolerance toward Jews. Jews had lived there for thousands of years, and the Jewish community in Rome was the oldest in the Western world. The first Jews in Rome had been brought as slaves but gradually gained their freedom. By the Middle Ages, Jews worked in many trades and occupations. Some esteemed Jewish physicians cared for Roman Catholic popes. By the late 1800s, the walls around Jewish ghettos in Rome and other cities had been torn down. Jews gained full civil rights and became part of all social and economic classes, as well as the various trades and professions.

By the early 1900s, anti-Semitism was not widespread in Italy, nor had it been part of dictator Benito Mussolini's original political agenda when he took charge in 1922. His government had support among various economic classes and religious groups. By the 1930s, thousands of Jews belonged to the Fascist Party. Furthermore, Mussolini expressed contempt toward Hitler's anti-Jewish policies and spoke scornfully about the German leader. There were no strong

Adolf Hitler and Benito Mussolini proclaim their alliance in 1940. Despite such sentiments, most Italians did not cooperate with the Nazis' anti-Semitic efforts.

groups of anti-Semitic Italians; few Fascist politicians favored actions against Jews.

But as Mussolini came to rely more and more on his German military ally, Hitler pressured him to pass discriminatory laws. In 1936, laws deprived Italian Jews of their jobs and positions in society, hitting middle-class people especially hard. Two years later, when Italy entered World War II as an ally of Nazi Germany, a second wave of persecution was launched, affecting more Jews. Yet, enforcement of these laws was often lax. Jews in Italy faced less persecution than any other European country dominated by the Nazis.

Starting in 1942, Hitler and his government complained bitterly that Italian officials resisted Nazi orders and local police thwarted efforts to arrest Jews. They insisted that Mussolini start deporting Jews to concentration camps. Mussolini hesitated. He worried about what would happen after the war to those who took part in Nazi brutality. He let Jewish relief organizations operate until 1943 when the German occupation began. These organizations played a crucial role, especially since many Jewish refugees from Germany and eastern Europe had fled to Italy.

Safe in the Italian Zone

Jews found refuge in regions occupied by Italian forces, such as the Italian Riviera, part of Greece, and southwestern Croatia, where Italian soldiers tried to stop the killings of Serbs and Jews. The Italian Foreign Ministry developed a policy of refusing to deliver Jews in these places to the Germans. Mussolini finally agreed to have Croatian Jews deported to death camps, but Italian authorities there found ways to thwart the plan. A high-ranking Italian officer in Croatia wrote, "We must keep the Italian Army from dirtying its hands with this business."

In 1941, Ivo Herzer and his parents, Yugoslavian Jews, were trying to flee from Nazi-occupied Croatia. Herzer recalls in *The Courage to Care*:

The train that we were travelling on got stuck, and we were ordered from the train with all the other passengers. We were in a no-win situation: We were stuck in the town of Gospic, where the Croatian fascist movement was born; we had no documents; there was a curfew for the Jews; and there was a concentration camp just outside town.

The family approached an Italian army sergeant, and Ivo's father, who knew a few words in Italian, said haltingly, "*Ehrei paura* [Jews fear]." The soldier replied, "Fear nothing." He managed to get the family and some other refugees on an Italian army train. From there they were taken across the border to Fiume, where the sergeant made sure they received food and drink. The Herzers stayed in the Italian zone until the war ended. They were among the thousands of Jews who survived with the help of Italian soldiers.

A false identification card issued by church authorities to a Croatian Jew living in Italy. Italians refused to give up Jews to the Nazi forces.

Fight for Survival

When Mussolini was deposed in July 1943, people hoped the war would soon end. Among other things, Italians were disturbed by stories of Nazi atrocities and they resented Nazi theories that Nordic peoples were "superior" to others. People celebrated in the streets when they heard the Allies had landed in Sicily. The new prime minister, Marshal Pietro Badoglio, signed an armistice with the Allies, and hope of war's end spread.

Instead, worse times began. In September 1943, German troops arrived in Italy and took control of the north, where most Jews lived. The Italian army was not strong enough to drive out the invaders. Badoglio surrendered after three days and Mussolini was installed at the head of a puppet regime in the north.

Most Italian police continued to refuse to cooperate with the Nazis and even worked against them. Among these Righteous Gentiles was police chief Mario di Nardis, who protected the Jews in his town, Aquila. Giovanni Palatucci, chief of police in Fiume, was arrested and killed in Dachau after he helped Jews in his town.

In Rome, police chief Mario de Marco was ordered to hand over lists of Jewish residents to the Nazis. He refused. De Marco secretly helped to provide Roman Jews with fake identity papers. The Gestapo arrested de Marco and tortured him to try to obtain the names of his colleagues, but he resisted. De Marco's courage saved hundreds of people from deportation and death.

Other Italian officials stalled or flatly refused German demands to deport Jews from Italy and places occupied by the Italian army. Some of them organized relief efforts and assisted priests who were hiding Jews. Some Italian officials supplied Jews with false identity papers that saved them from Nazi roundups.

On September 10, Hitler had said Rome would remain an "open city," but German soldiers soon appeared and declared martial law. As the Germans approached Rome, shops in the Jewish neighborhood were closed and people stayed behind locked doors, waiting and worrying. Some listened furtively to the radio. At that point, writes Gianni di Veroli, Rome seemed to fall into two parts: "those who went into hiding and those who were helping them."[78]

In the months that followed, Jews all over Italy would rely on Righteous Gentiles for their very lives. On September 26, Heinrich Himmler informed Herbert Kappler, the German SS commander in Rome, that all Jews were to be "transferred to Germany and liquidated."[79] This should be a surprise, said Himmler, with no warning or prior actions to alert people.

Kappler first announced that Rome's Jews could ransom their lives by paying the Germans 50 kilos (110 pounds) of gold. The Jewish community had no idea where to find this large amount. People scraped together whatever they could and sold possessions to buy gold at exorbitant prices on the black market. On the day the gold was collected, a number of Christians came to the synagogue to contribute. One woman, who asked to remain anonymous, brought Jewish leaders numerous heavy gold coins.

For the Nazis, this ransom was just a way to rob Jews of any remaining wealth before deporting them. On October 13, Nazis stole priceless historical documents and art objects from the ancient Roman synagogue. Three days later came the Black Sabbath raid.

Jews who escaped the raid looked for places to hide. People could be seen running along rooftops, throwing crying children out of windows to adults waiting to catch them on the street below. Those who could not get away were thrust onto trucks without mercy—hungry infants, old men, a half-paralyzed woman in her wheelchair.

Among those who fled from their homes were Enrico and Grazia Di Veroli and their four children. The family had been awakened the morning of October 16 when a neighborhood child rang their doorbell and cried, "Hurry, the Germans are coming!"[80] With raincoats over their nightclothes, they left their apartment one at a time.

The Di Verolis found refuge in the home of Catholics they knew in Rome's Trastavere quarter. This very poor family shared their small food rations with the Di Verolis and the woman gave up her bed for the children. Michele di Enrico, one of the children, recalled, "A lot of the people in the neighborhood knew we were Jews, and one person would bring us something to eat, another would bring something else, so that we didn't have to go out and risk being seen."[81]

However, the family had to leave again after someone told the Germans they were there. The Di Verolis left just as Nazi police were arriving. They found refuge at a convent, but after only ten days the Nazis came there, too. Enrico's daughter Olga remembers, "In this convent, along with Jews, there were a number of soldiers and officers who had escaped from the Italian army. The people in the convent tried to help as much as possible, but they had to send us away."[82]

Next, they went to the home of one of their father's former business clients, where they were warmly welcomed, fed well, and urged to sleep in the family's best rooms. But one night, Jews were arrested outside this house, so the family fled again. Olga's two brothers, Michele and Gianni, joined the anti-Fascist resistance, while the rest of the family went to stay in some buildings connected with the Church of San Benedetto. By the war's end, the Di Verolis had been hidden in seven different places. All but Enrico escaped deportation and death.

Aid from the Clergy

Throughout the war, Jews and others criticized Pope Pius XII for not speaking out forcefully against the Nazi persecution and murder of Jews and for not making it clear that any Catholics who took part in such acts would be excommunicated, or cut off from the sacraments of the church. Some historians believe that church leaders thought Hitler would not allow the churches

Pope Pius XII refused to condemn Nazi actions against the Jews.

to function at all if they took a more defiant stance.

Yet hundreds of individual bishops, priests, monks, and nuns helped Jews. People in need often trusted clergy more than other strangers and so turned to them for help. Clergy also knew many other people who could aid fugitives. To help Jews avoid Nazi persecution and deportations, the clergy issued thousands of papers falsely verifying baptism, or Christian conversion, before 1938. Jews were hidden in convents, monasteries, and inside the Vatican itself. Hundreds of Jews hid in the Instituto Angelo Mai, a Catholic religious institute. The pope knew about these activities. In fact, one of the most energetic rescuers operated under his nose.

The "Scarlet Pimpernel" of the Vatican: Hugh O'Flaherty

Monsignor Hugh Joseph O'Flaherty, known for his compassion, humor, and love of golf, was among the most active rescuers in Italy. This Irish-born priest hid thousands of people, some inside Vatican City, others throughout Rome. Besides Jews, he saved many Allied soldiers who had escaped from the Germans.

To carry out his work, O'Flaherty helped to produce false documents and traded in the black market when necessary. He did not hide from the Nazis but stood boldly on the steps of St. Peter's Basilica in the Vatican, where people in need could find him. One day in 1943, shortly after the Nazis arrived in Rome, a Jewish man approached him and spoke as he furtively revealed a heavy gold chain wrapped around his waist:

My wife and I expect to be arrested at any moment. We have no way of escaping. When we are taken to Germany we shall die. But we have a small son, he is only seven and too young to die in a Nazi gas chamber. Please take this chain and take the boy for us too. Each link on this chain will keep him alive for a month. Will you at least save him?[83]

Monsignor O'Flaherty assured the man that he would find a safe place for his son. Furthermore, he would help the man and his wife by supplying them with false identity papers. At the end of the war, all three were alive. O'Flaherty returned the man's gold chain, saying, "I did not need it."[84]

Several times during the occupation, the Gestapo tried to capture O'Flaherty. The priest was safe as long as he stayed behind a white line that marked the border of Vatican City, a place the Nazis had agreed not to invade. But O'Flaherty managed to leave sometimes in a disguise, often as a peasant.

O'Flaherty expressed outrage at Nazi brutality. When he saw the Germans herding captive Jews onto trucks, he said the Nazis treated "these gentle people like beasts."[85] As more Italians saw this brutality, O'Flaherty found an increasing number of willing helpers for his rescue work.

Safe in Assisi

In the hilly town of Assisi, Padre Rufino Niccacci, the head of the seminary of Saint Damiano, led a rescue network that successfully hid about three hundred Jews in religious buildings, mostly monasteries and convents.

Shortly after Rome fell to the Nazis, the bishop of Assisi, Giuseppe Nicolini, had asked the thirty-two-year-old Niccacci to help Jews. The bishop called for him in the middle of the night and said, "I want you to take care of some refugees who are now sleeping under my roof."[86] As the conversation continued, Bishop Nicolini explained, "They are not ordinary refugees. They are Jews who escaped from Rome today. There is a rabbi among them."[87] Niccacci was directed to escort these ten people, who were posing as Christian pilgrims, early the next morning to Florence.

This mission completed, Niccacci and a group of priests, nuns, and local residents went on to help other Jews who came to Assisi. All of these Jews were strangers when they arrived. Assisi had never before had Jewish residents. Niccacci set up two schools, one for the academic instruction of Jewish children, the other to help Jews understand enough about Catholic practices to fool the Nazis. He helped them to practice their own religion and celebrate Jewish holidays whenever possible.

This work became extremely risky as German soldiers spread throughout Italy, imposing martial law on local people and installing Nazi police. When they arrived in Assisi, the Germans demanded that the mayor turn over some hostages who could be kept as "insurance." These hostages would be killed in retaliation if any locals attacked or killed a German. The mayor refused and resigned his position in protest. The Nazis searched regularly for Jews, resistance members, and escaped Allied soldiers, now entering monasteries and convents, once exempt from such raids.

For help, Niccacci called upon local residents he could trust. One of them was an

Padre Rufino Niccacci (center) led a rescue network that hid approximately three hundred Jews in monasteries and convents.

A View of the "Just World"

Prisoners who managed to survive the concentration camp at Auschwitz-Birkenau have called it "hell on earth." At age twenty-four, in 1944, Primo Levi, a Jewish chemist from Turin, Italy, was interned in this death camp. About 90 percent of the people in the group with whom he arrived died within days, either from gassing, starvation, or illness.

Levi was relieved: Assigned to work in a synthetic rubber company on camp grounds operated by the German conglomerate I. G. Farben, he was less exposed to the elements and able to smuggle out items to trade for extra food. Nevertheless, only about one-third of the inmates assigned to work with the hazardous chemicals and machinery in this factory survived brutal conditions and guards.

Under these circumstances, people not only suffered terribly but lost faith in human nature. In his book *Survival in Auschwitz*, Levi describes how his sense of hopelessness was eased by Lorenzo Perrone. Perrone was a kindly bricklayer who had been brought to the camp as a forced laborer, though not as an inmate. Levi began talking with him after realizing that Perrone came from the same region of Italy. Civilian workers were forbidden to speak with prisoners, but Perrone disobeyed. Every day, Perrone brought Levi some extra bread, soup, and other food. He gave him a vest to help protect him from the cold. On Levi's behalf, he sent a postcard to Italy and brought back the response.

Later, Levi would say, "It was really due to Lorenzo that I am alive today; not so much for his material aid, as for his having constantly reminded me by his presence, by his natural and plain manner of being good, that there still existed a just world outside our own."

By behaving humanely, Perrone had reminded Levi that there was goodness left in a world that seemed utterly evil. Levi was able to maintain his own feelings of being human. He later found out that Perrone had helped others, not just Italians, and that he had refused to accept any rewards for his acts.

elderly local printer, Luigi Brizi. During their meeting, Brizi asked, "How can I help?" Niccacci replied, "By printing false identity cards in your printing shop. By contributing to the cause you preach yourself—freedom and democracy. . . . By saving their lives."[88] Using samples the priest gave him, Brizi printed cards that would transform Jews into Catholics. Other people added names, photos, seals, and stamps to make these papers look authentic. The group would eventually make hundreds of cards for Jews throughout the region. By night, the printer and his son Trento did this hazardous work; by day, Luigi ran his print shop as usual, sometimes selling postcards to German soldiers who came by.

It was dangerous to have large numbers of Jews hiding in local monasteries and other buildings, so the priests took many of them out of the country. In one daring rescue, Niccacci led a group of Jews out of Assisi to the side of the Italian front that was controlled by the Allies. Niccacci took several groups to Florence en route to Genoa. From there, they would flee the country. In November 1943, while Niccacci was in Florence, he witnessed a massive Nazi raid on that city during which one thousand Jews were arrested at gunpoint and some were gunned down for trying to escape. At a Carmine convent the Nazis had taken away fifty Jewish orphans in hiding. Only two were saved: The mother superior had managed to hide these little girls under her clothing.

Assisi was raided by the Nazis, but informers at Gestapo headquarters warned the villagers before the raids occurred. The priests and other townspeople helped Jews to hide in the mountains and forests until the danger passed. During another emergency, the priests hid people in private homes and in Roman ruins on the grounds of the bishop's palace.

Early in 1944, the Gestapo arrested Niccacci and imprisoned him at Perugia, where he was interrogated and sentenced to die. Church leaders managed to bribe the Nazis for his release, along with that of some other prisoners.

On April 29, 1974, Padre Rufino Niccacci was honored by Yad Vashem. The sixty-three-year-old monk planted a carob sapling along the Avenue of the Righteous. At the ceremony that followed, many of the refugees he had helped paid tribute to this courageous man.

"They Are Innocents": Rescuers in Genoa

Genoa and Milan were two cities in which many Jews found help. Jews in Milan had set up a committee known as Comasebit, later called Delasem, to help refugees. Its director was a Jewish attorney named Lelio Vittorio Valobra. In September 1943, as the Germans invaded Italy and banned Delasem and similar organizations, Valobra met with

"They Did Everything to Help Me"

Paulette Pomeranz was seven years old in 1941 when her region of Greece, Salonika, came under Nazi control. Two years later, Germany gained control of the whole country. Pomeranz lived with a Greek family under the care of the grandmother, a woman named Julia. She later told author Maxine B. Rosenberg, "The townspeople were frightened. . . . Although I was the only Jewish person in the neighborhood, they knew that if the Germans found me, we'd all be shot. Yet they did everything to help me." For example, a baker figured out an escape route Paulette could use in case of danger.

Food shortages became so severe that the family sometimes had only raisins to eat. Paulette worried that one or more townspeople might become desperate enough to turn her in for food. However, she survived the war and later moved to America with her mother.

The two families stayed in touch. Julia decided to move to the United States in 1958 after she had visited Paulette's family. They remained close until Julia died in 1993. Paulette Pomeranz later said, "She gave me a home and affection and kept me safe. I could never repay her for what she had done."

the archbishop of Genoa, Pietro Cardinal Boetto, who had shown compassion for Jews. Valobra warned them there was danger ahead. A year earlier, Italian officers had told Boetto about the atrocities being committed against Jews in eastern Europe.

Hearing these things, the cardinal and his assistant, Father Francesco Repetto, were immediately in agreement: They would aid the Jews, taking over the work that had been done by Delasem. Cardinal Boetto said, "They are innocents; they are in great danger; we must help them at whatever cost to ourselves."[89]

Repetto and Boetto created a rescue network of nuns, monks, and priests throughout northern Italy. Boetto deeply respected the chief rabbi of Genoa, Riccardo Pacifici, who had stayed in the city to minister to Jews and refugees. Refugees were invited to share Sabbath meals with Pacifici and his family, and the rabbi often visited the prison at Calabria to minister to those who were confined there. This learned man, the author of several books, organized a school, study groups, a cafeteria, and outings. Boetto found a hiding place for Rabbi Pacifici from which he could continue his ministry yet remain safe from the Nazis.

By the end of 1943, Repetto was running an extensive rescue network in the region. He found trustworthy people to carry messages, shelter and feed refugees, and provide documents and money. He also located guides to take refugees to safety in Switzerland. In July 1944, Repetto was forced to go into hiding himself to elude the Gestapo. Other Genoans carried on with the rescue work.

Describing rescues in Italy, author Susan Zuccotti writes:

> The postwar testimony of Italian Jews reveals many varieties in the pattern of survival. Many . . . survivors write of the simple people who helped them— peasants, maids, janitors who hid them in attics or cellars, or saved their possessions. Other survivors . . . write movingly of help from a lawyer, doctor, bishop, or bureaucrat. Survivors lived in cities and villages, in convents and isolated farmhouses.[90]

Through these efforts, nearly 85 percent of Italy's Jews survived the war, a reversal of the estimates for Europe as a whole: 80 percent of the Jews who lived on the continent before the war were killed.

Righteous Gentiles in Hungary, Romania, Bulgaria, and Yugoslavia

Anti-Semitism was prevalent in eastern and central Europe. During World War II, Romanian Jews were the victims of barbaric attacks, including a massacre of twelve thousand Jews in 1941 in Iasi, located in northern Romania.

Jews in Hungary had experienced less persecution than in some other countries. During the early 1900s, many Jews became prominent educators, scientists, political leaders, writers, and artists. Violence against Hungarian Jews and their property was rare, although Jews faced certain legal restrictions and quotas at schools and universities.

Anti-Semitism increased after World War I, and Jews were subjected to more violence during the early 1920s. By the 1930s, the fascist militia group Arrow Cross claimed many Hungarian members. More hate propaganda against Jews appeared in magazines and newspapers. The government, under Admiral Miklos Horthy, became allied with Germany, part of the Axis that included Italy and Japan.

Even so, the Horthy government refrained from deporting Hungarian Jews, and many Jews from neighboring countries viewed Hungary as a fairly safe haven. That situation changed drastically in 1944. In October, German troops occupied Hungary. Horthy was replaced with Ferenc Szalasi, a man Hitler trusted to carry out the deportation of Jews to death camps. To speed up this process, the Reich Central Security Office's expert on Jewish affairs, Adolf Eichmann, went to Hungary. Although Germany was now losing the war, top-ranking Nazis were determined to kill as many Jews as possible before the Allies arrived. In the months that followed, half the Jews of Hungary (two hundred thousand) would die at Auschwitz-Birkenau.

In their efforts to locate and round up Jews, the Nazis received help from members of the Arrow Cross and other collaborators.

Jews in Hungary in 1945. The photographer who took this photo claimed that the couple feared him, refusing to believe the Nazis had been defeated.

Jews found help wherever they could—sometimes from a policeman who opposed the Nazis. Among them was Alfred Miller, who stored food that he gave to the Jewish underground and used to feed starving Jewish orphans.

Other Jews were aided by the clergy, both Catholic and Protestant. Jews were hidden in monasteries, convents, and foreign missions. One of these survivors was Andy Sterling, who was born in 1935 and lived in Nagykata, a town in Hungary not far from Budapest. Sterling later described how he was hidden in a Catholic orphanage in October 1944:

My parents said I'd be going to a Catholic orphanage in Budapest with Paul, their friend's child, who was two years older than I. Paul's parents had found the place, and the priest in charge was willing to hide us. [My sister], now five, was being sent to a convent, and my mother was going to live with a Catholic family in town.[91]

Eight other Jewish boys were also hidden in the orphanage at the time. By November, Allied bombings were becoming so frequent that the children and the priests had to spend virtually all of their time in the bunkers for shelter, where they tried to carry on with their school lessons. The priests went outside to get whatever food they could find for the boys, since the only thing left in the pantry was some corn. In January 1945 the Russians liberated the country and Sterling was reunited with his parents and sister. Using false identity papers, his father had managed to survive in the outside world, working as an ambulance driver. Sterling never forgot the kind priest who had sheltered him and the other boys. He says, "I learned from him

what it means to give, and today I try to lead that kind of life."[92]

A number of other Jews were helped by courageous individuals like Valeriu Moldovan.

"He Risked His Life": Valeriu Moldovan

Solomon Fleischman was sixteen years old in 1944 when the Nazis began rounding up Hungarian Jews, first isolating them in ghettos from which they would be sent to death camps. Solomon recalls:

Realizing that our family [which included 11 children] was too large to hide together, we had to split up. My father gathered his children around him and told us to scatter and somehow try to live through this. . . . Then he took out all his money and divided it up among us. Even my infant sister had money tucked in her clothes in the hope that a kind Gentile might rescue her.[93]

Left to his own devices, the teenage Solomon dashed into a cellar beneath the apartment building where his family lived, bringing candles, blankets, and bread. One of his uncles was already hiding there when he arrived. Above them were small businesses, including a barbershop and carpentry shop.

When they ran out of food, Fleischman asked the fourteen-year-old carpenter's apprentice from the shop above to bring some, using Solomon's ration coupons. The boy agreed, and the men in hiding survived this way for three weeks. Then, one day, they were dismayed when a man opened the cellar door. It was Valeriu Moldovan, the Romanian-born owner of the carpentry shop and father of two small children. "Come out, I know you're here," he called out to them. "Don't worry, I'll take care of you."[94]

Moldovan kept that promise. Refusing to accept any payment, he brought Fleischman and his uncle food and kept them informed about what was happening outside. Disaster struck when two workers discovered the Jews' hiding place. They suggested to Moldovan that the three of them turn the men in and collect the reward money, but Moldovan talked them out of it.

Another Christian neighbor saved Fleischman with her quick thinking. One day, a detective spotted him outside the hiding place and later returned to unlock the cellar door and investigate. This woman convinced the detective that the boy he had seen was the carpenter's apprentice, an orphan who came by on weekends to use the washroom in the shop.

Late in 1944, Russian troops liberated the town and people in hiding were finally free. Solomon Fleischman discovered that he was the only member of his immediate family to survive the war. He later moved to America and became the father of five children and seventeen grandchildren. Solomon gratefully acknowledged the righteous Romanian who saved him, sending him and his family money and gifts in the years after the war. He says, "More than once, Moldovan risked his life to protect us."[95]

"We'll Do What We Can": Malka Csizmadia

Malka Csizmadia was seventeen years old when the Nazis built a ghetto in her small Hungarian village, Satoraljaujhely. As time went on, they conducted raids and seized Jewish residents, some of whom were her family's friends. When she walked around the neighborhood and saw the abandoned homes, with food still on the tables and chil-

dren's toys strewn on the floor, Malka Csizmadia felt horror and sorrow.

Weeks later, she encountered a Jewish man in an enclosed work camp and offered to help him. First, she delivered letters for him, then brought back newspapers and other things he needed. She let the man use her home address to receive mail. When her mother asked what she was doing, Malka told her. They decided they would both help the people in the camp. Her mother agreed that it was the right thing to do.

The family began sending and receiving mail for several men trapped in the camp. They also brought them food. When it became clear in 1944 that the Russian troops were moving into Hungary soon, they feared the retreating Germans might kill their captives or march them by force to camps in Germany. They decided to help hide as many men as they could. Malka recalls, "We had plans to take as many men as we could to nearby farms where people had agreed to hide them in their wheat."[96]

The designated day was cold and rainy. Malka, her mother, and her sister escorted some of the men. Malka set out first with a man who was disguised as a woman with a bandage over his beard. She recalls the events that followed:

> We decided to walk separately because it was safer. When a soldier stopped me to ask me where I was going, I said, "to the village to get bread." I would distract them by giving them cigarettes so [the first Jewish man] could sneak by. We finally reached the farm. My mother wasn't there yet, but she came in half an hour. My mother and I went back and forth bringing food, and my sister and mother brought about twenty more men from hiding place to hiding place. We continued this for about five weeks until the Russians liberated our area.[97]

Thanks to the efforts of these three compassionate women, twenty-five men survived to celebrate the liberation of Hungary early in 1945.

Hiding in Yugoslavia

After the Nazis occupied Yugoslavia in 1941, Hitler divided the country into two sections, Serbia and Croatia. That July, when the Nazis entered Croatia, Samuel and Erna Nachmias and their three children fled to a seaside town in Yugoslavia where Italian troops were in control and Jews were not harmed. Then, in September 1943, the Italians were overcome by German troops, and Jews in this region faced persecution and death. The Germans posted notices in public places announcing that anyone who hid Jews would face the death penalty.

Olga Bartulovic had met the Nachmias family during a period of some months when they were all living in the same house. She advised them not to register as Jews when the Nazis first made this demand; then, she helped them obtain false papers and hide in a convent. After Nazis began searching this place, Bartulovic and her sister-in-law Dragica moved the family members to safe territory, one at a time.

Erna Nachmias later said, "Olga Bartulovic and her sister-in-law Dragica were prompted in their actions by purely humane considerations, deriving no personal benefit or gain. In doing what they did, they exposed themselves to mortal danger."[98]

Ivan Vranetic, a religious Catholic, was only fifteen years old when he began hiding Jews in 1942. His family lived in Topusko, on the border of Bosnia. Vranetic later recalled how he began his rescue work:

> The first was a twenty-year-old man from Sarajevo who was hiding from the Germans and the Partisans because he didn't want to be drafted. His entire family had been killed, and he was weak and sick and he didn't want to be killed, too. He had no shoes, nothing, and when he told me his story I had to help him. I think it must be my upbringing, because I had seen people who were homeless and I had feelings in my heart that I had to help.[99]

Soon word spread in the area that Jews who needed help could go to Vranetic. Erna

Montilio, one of the people he helped, recalls that after she arrived in Topusko, other Jews told her, "There's this young man here named Ivan, and he helps everybody. He gives us a place to stay, helps us find food."[100]

Erna was with her mother, sister, and two-year-old baby. Vranetic could not find a safe hiding place for all of them, so he brought them to his own home. When the Germans were conducting their raids, Vranetic went about warning people, then helped them to survive in the forest where they had to hide. Sometimes, he escorted them to safe hiding places in the woods and hid with them. To keep warm, these people

Fifteen-year-old Ivan Vranetic started hiding Jews at his home in 1942. When Germans threatened his home with raids, Vranetic hid Jews in the forest, aiding them with food and supplies.

had to cover themselves with newspapers. But they did survive, and in 1964, many of them came to honor Ivan Vranetic when he received his medal from Yad Vashem.

"Savior-Angel": Raoul Wallenberg

In the face of relentless brutality, one man organized a rescue effort every bit as relentless. The heroic Swedish diplomat Raoul Wallenberg was able to save tens of thousands of Jews in Budapest.

Wallenberg was born in 1912 to a wealthy, influential family that included politicians, diplomats, industrialists, and bankers. Raoul was expected to work in the family's international banking business but chose to study architecture. He excelled in this field at the University of Michigan where he earned his college degree.

After Wallenberg graduated in 1935, he worked in South Africa, then in Palestine where he met Jewish refugees. He liked to tell people that he had some Jewish ancestry—his grandmother's grandfather was one of the first Jews in Sweden. When he returned home, Wallenberg joined a specialty food import-export company. His partner, Koloman Lauer, was a Hungarian Jew. Wallenberg traveled throughout Europe as international director of this company.

Like many others, Wallenberg became aware of Nazi brutality toward Jews. By 1944, eyewitnesses had told the world about the atrocities being committed in the death camps. Most of Europe's Jewish communities had been destroyed; now, the Nazis set out to deport the Jews of Hungary, beginning with those in rural areas.

The United States had set up the War Refugee Board (WRB) to save Jews. WRB officials met with a committee in neutral Sweden to discuss the rescue of Hungarian Jews.

Koloman Lauer, a member of this committee, believed Wallenberg was well suited to lead this effort—he cared deeply about people, spoke several languages, and was energetic and resourceful. The committee approved Wallenberg, who said, "I will do it gladly if I can help people in need."[101]

In June 1944, Wallenberg arrived in Hungary with a diplomatic title, staff, and generous funding from the WRB. By then, 230,000 of about 670,000 Hungarian Jews remained, most of them in Budapest. Wallenberg began his rescue effort by hiring hundreds of Jews to work with his group. To create "safe houses" for Jews, the Swedes bought or rented buildings and gave them names like Swedish Research Institute or Red Cross, with a Swedish flag displayed outside. They set up clinics, soup kitchens, and children's shelters.

Wallenberg's people also distributed protective passports, impressive-looking papers he had designed himself. Within weeks, they had issued thousands of passes. Wallenberg kept issuing more, designating bearers as subject to Swedish immunity via family or official ties with Sweden. Other neutral governments began issuing passes, too.

For a while, roundups of Jews stopped; Eichmann left Hungary. Then, in October, the Nazis overthrew the government and installed a Hungarian Nazi, Ferenc Szalasi, as leader. Attacks on Jews resumed.

In response, Wallenberg stepped up his rescue work, issuing more passes and setting up new safe houses. Inspired by his example, the Swiss and Vatican governments also opened more safe houses. As the Nazis began deporting people, Wallenberg snatched them out of lines and even off trains. At times, he used bribes, threats, and bluffs to save people. On several occasions, he told the Nazis they had taken "his" people and authoritatively demanded their release. People whom he rescued said that Wallenberg would go to the railroad station and call out, "Which of you has documents in Hungarian proving that you once held a valid Swedish pass? . . . Present those documents to me at once!" As people held out ration cards, tax forms, and various other papers, Wallenberg would examine them, saying, "Yes, that shows you had a pass. . . . Yes, obviously you had one, too. . . . You too."[102]

He passed out food, medicine, and clothing to people when he saw groups being marched out of the city. When the Nazis invaded the Swedish houses to seize Jews, Wallenberg risked his life, saying, "You will have to shoot me first."[103]

Using his official position as a diplomat, Raoul Wallenberg committed himself to saving the Jews of Hungary.

SCHUTZ-PASS

Nr. 46/75

Name: Frau Alexander Flamm
Név: geb. Gizella Szántó

Wohnort: Budaest
Lakás:

Geburtsdatum: 3. Dezember 1913.
Születési ideje:

Geburtsort: Budapest
Születési helye:

Körperlänge: 160 cm
Magasság:

Haarfarbe: schwarz   **Augenfarbe:** braun
Hajszín: **Szemszín:**
Georg Thomas Flamm 3.2.1940.Bpest
Stefan Johann Flamm 24.12.1941.

Unterschrift:
Aláírás:

SCHWEDEN   SVÉDORSZÁG

A Swedish Schutz-Pass of the type Wallenberg had printed in the thousands.

During the last months of the war, Budapest was in chaos. Groups of Arrow Cross terrorized Jews who remained in the city. Bombs rained down from Allied planes. One survivor later said that Wallenberg continued to fight the Nazis and to bring people food, medicine, and hope: "In the complete and total hell in which we lived, there was a savior-angel somewhere, moving around."[104] Wallenberg even convinced German soldiers to stop the Arrow Cross from killing Jews, or face harsh criminal penalties after the war.

The famous concert violinist Victor Aitay had escaped from a labor camp and made his way back to Budapest where he received one of Wallenberg's passes and was given a job working at the switchboard in the Swedish embassy. He later recalled:

One day in December 1944, [the Arrow Cross] came into the embassy and took 200 or 250 people. This was supposed to be a Swedish sanctuary but there was no such thing as law anymore. Whoever they took, they would shoot at the edge

During the chaos that reigned in bombed-out Hungary at the end of the war, Raoul Wallenberg disappeared. Although the cause of his disappearance remains a mystery, he is thought to have died in a Russian prison years after being arrested by the Soviets.

of the Danube; that was the usual procedure. I called the number I had in case of emergencies, and two hours later, every single person who had been taken was back. . . . To this day, I don't know who was on the other end of the telephone, but whoever it was had power over even the Arrow Cross. That's how high an in Wallenberg had. He had contact with [Adolf] Eichmann, with everybody. He was simply not afraid.[105]

Convinced that the Russians would soon free Hungary, Wallenberg wrote to his mother about the coming peace and his long-awaited return home. There were about 144,000 Jews left in Budapest when Russian troops arrived in February 1945. Wallenberg felt his work was not done: He arranged to meet with a Russian commander to discuss ways to help Hungarian Jews after their terrible ordeal.

However, during this meeting, Wallenberg was taken into custody and subsequently disappeared. In the years that followed, people tried to find out where he had been taken and why. At that time, the Russian government under Joseph Stalin

Tributes to a Missing Hero

Swedish diplomat Raoul Wallenberg is credited with saving more Jews during the Holocaust than any other individual. His mysterious disappearance in 1945, when he was only thirty-three years old, deprived Wallenberg of the hero's welcome and the life he might have enjoyed after the war. Instead, he suffered loneliness, deprivation, and probably despair inside the dreaded Soviet prison system known as the Gulag. The Soviets may have thought Wallenberg was a spy. Or perhaps they feared he would thwart their plans to make Hungary part of the postwar Communist bloc in Eastern Europe.

Victor Aitay was a Hungarian Jew who was working in the Swedish embassy under Wallenberg's protection. He later said:

> I was still at the embassy when Wallenberg left. He always left with a backpack, always in a hurry, a million things on his mind, running and running and saving and saving. The day he left, we didn't know where he was going. Nobody knew what was going to happen.

Despite pressure from several governments and the efforts of the Raoul Wallenberg Associations, he has not been freed, nor has his body been returned to his family. Wallenberg's mother died in 1979 at age eighty-seven, still grieving for her lost son.

Raoul Wallenberg has not been forgotten. A street and monument in Budapest bear his name. The Raoul Wallenberg Associations sponsor education programs to promote tolerance and compassion and condemn the hate and bigotry that exploded into the Holocaust.

During the 1980s, Wallenberg was made an honorary citizen of the United States, Canada, and Israel. Senator Tom Lantos of California spearheaded this act in the U.S. Congress. Born in Budapest in 1928, Lantos had lived with his family in one of Wallenberg's protected houses in 1944 while he worked with the underground. In 1997, the United States issued a commemorative stamp to honor the Righteous Gentile Raoul Wallenberg.

Raoul Wallenberg's heroic efforts are recognized by a 1997 stamp issued in the United States.

A Stubborn "Ally"

Bulgaria was allied with Germany, yet efforts to persecute Jews did not succeed there. Near the end of 1942, the Nazis set out to identify Bulgarian Jews, the first step in persecuting them. The people of Bulgaria—in its government, royal family, churches, and citizenry—opposed these efforts. In May 1943, members of the Parliament stood up to protest the deportation of Bulgarian Jews. Church leaders announced that they would open their doors to Jews who wanted sanctuary. If Jews were deported, said these clergy, their members would join them.

The Bulgarians also resisted anti-Jewish laws. Gentiles joined Jews in wearing yellow armbands after the Germans issued this order in their country. Sabotage and resistance prevented the Nazis from carrying out plans to deport Jews from old Bulgaria, although the Nazis were able to deport Jews from Thrace and Macedonia, new Bulgarian territories. Instead of sending Bulgarian Jews to Polish concentration camps as they had planned, the Nazis settled for having Jews removed from the capital, Sofia, and taken to the country.

The five thousand Jews who lived in old Bulgaria survived the Holocaust. Shabtay Levy told authors Leora Kahn and Rachel Hager:

> One-quarter or one-third of Sofia was destroyed [by bombs], but because of the evacuation, there were no Jews there. We'd all left. That was a twist of luck. After the war, three thousand Nazis and collaborators were executed in Bulgaria. Within a year it was done. And all the confiscated property was returned to the Jews.

imprisoned many people without a fair hearing or trial. In 1957 the Russians declared that Wallenberg had died in prison in 1947. Yet ex-prisoners reported seeing him in different prisons and also in a Russian mental hospital as late as the 1970s. The official Soviet story remained unchanged. The fate of this courageous humanitarian remains a mystery.

Beacons of Hope

When the war ended, people moved on to rebuild their lives. Most rescuers said little if anything about their activities during the Holocaust. Their actions remained private, sometimes unknown even to their children. Many felt like Belgian rescuer Esta Heiber, who says, "For an entire generation you couldn't talk about the war because you couldn't live if you talked about it. If you remained in those memories you couldn't live. . . . The war changed me completely. I can't even remember who I was before the war." [106]

The war left many people in ruined health, emotionally scarred. Living in fear for long periods of time took its toll. A number of rescuers endured recurring nightmares, depression, anxiety, and other signs of stress. Some, especially in postwar Eastern Europe, also had to endure ostracism and persecution from anti-Semites in their communities. Many were living in poverty.

Among those who struggled with painful memories were Dutch rescuers Miep and Jan Gies. Each year, on the day the Franks were arrested, the Gieses spent the day inside their home, sitting in silent sorrow.

Some rescuers had suffered grievous losses. Louisa Steenstra was left a widow, her young daughter fatherless. The Nazis had viciously murdered her husband Albert when he refused to tell them where Jews were hidden inside their home. John Weidner, whose rescue network Dutch-Paris saved more than eight hundred Jews, mourned for his sister Gabrielle. When the Nazis found out that she was part of the network, they sent her to a concentration camp, where she was killed. Weidner recalled this event whenever he saw the church where she had been arrested. He himself had been tortured by the Nazis before he managed to escape. The beatings left him with permanent head injuries. Of his fellow rescuers, Weidner says, "Many have died before their time." [107]

Some rescuers viewed the war years as a time of tremendous personal growth. Helping others, despite such enormous obstacles, had brought them personal satisfaction. They felt stronger inside and more self-confident as they went on to tackle new challenges.

Many rescuers continued to actively help others. Their lives after the war reflected the strong concern for justice they had shown during the Holocaust. Some chose careers in helping professions such as social work, nursing, and child care. They volunteered to help children, the poor, the homeless, the elderly, and others in their communities. They became involved in groups that promote international peace and civil rights. They continued to fight against racism and intolerance toward people of different religions and ethnic groups.

Contact Between Rescuers and Rescued

After the war, a number of rescuers heard from the people they had helped, and some had regular or occasional contact. French rescuer Raoul Laporterie cherished a collection of letters he received from the grateful people he "passed" safely. Some people arranged meetings, either in their homelands or in other places, often in the United States or Israel. In 1988, Belgian rescuer Marie Taquet was honored at a reunion attended by many of the eighty Jews, now adult men, whom she had hidden inside a school.

Some rescuers felt a special connection with the Jewish people and decided to move to Israel. A number of others, including Aart and Johtje Vos, left behind the sad memories of their homelands to start new lives in America or other countries.

Lola Reichler (first from right) poses with her rescuer, Albina Zimmerman, in 1963. After the war, a number of rescuers were reunited with the Jews they helped to save.

Many grateful survivors remembered their rescuers after the war. Several Jewish families settled in Assisi, Italy, center of a famous rescue network, and became part of the community. Prosperous survivors aided poor residents and contributed funds for Bishop Nicolini's charitable work. They donated money for a Catholic orphanage run by Padre Niccacci in Trevi. Luigi Brizi was presented with a new printing press. Gino Battaglia, who had served the Assisi underground as a cyclist-courier, won the Tour de France on his new bicycle. Says Alexander Ramati, author of a book about the Assisi underground, "Those Jews whose lives had been saved, just like their Christian benefactors, were imbued with the idea that we are all our brother's keepers."[108]

Some Jews helped rescuers emigrate from their homelands, where they were being persecuted, or to places where they could get a fresh start. For example, funding from a Jewish relief group helped Oskar and Emilie Schindler move to Argentina.

Alone, Schindler returned to Germany in 1958. When his postwar business failed, Schindler relied upon people he had saved for support. He visited some of them in Israel for a few months every year. In 1963 Schindler became the third person honored as a Righteous Gentile. It was noted that he had rescued Jews over a fairly long period of time and on a large scale. When Schindler died in 1974, he was buried in a Catholic cemetery on Mount Zion in Jerusalem. On his tombstone were engraved these words: "The unforgettable life savior of 1,200 oppressed Jews."

Recognition for the Righteous

Righteous Gentiles have been honored and recognized by their own communities and countries, as well as other nations. For some, such tributes occurred soon after the war; for others, it took decades.

The first large-scale effort to honor Righteous Gentiles came in 1953 with the establishment of Yad Vashem. At the Yad Vashem Memorial in Jerusalem, people can mourn and remember the millions of victims of the Holocaust. They can also walk along the Avenue of the Righteous as they recall how some people worked against this evil.

The committee that confers the title of Righteous Gentile reviews new applications from people who wish to give testimony on behalf of a rescuer. Despite the strict standards used to verify these heroic acts, the list of people honored by Yad Vashem has steadily grown each year.

The year 1953 also marked the planting of a forest in northern Israel to honor Dutch rescuer Joop Westerweel. A few years later, on November 6, 1957, a large group of survivors and their rescuers met in New York City where the Anti-Defamation League of the B'nai B'rith dedicated a memorial to "Christian Heroes who helped their Jewish Brethren escape the Nazi terror." A rescuer from France, Madame Marie Helene Lefaucheux, unveiled the plaque. During the war, Lefaucheux had helped Father Pierre Chaillet save hundreds of Jewish children from the Nazis.

In 1959, the Jewish community of Italy gave gold medals to Christians who had played important roles in rescuing Jews. Monsignor Montini (later Pope Paul VI), head of the Holy See's Aid Service to Refugees during the war, declined to accept a medal. He said, "I acted in the line of duty and for that I am not entitled to a medal." [109]

Some of the people honored by Yad Vashem have also declined medals or material aid. They claim that they did what they should have done and that doing the right

Oskar Schindler stands near a tree planted in his honor at Yad Vashem in Jerusalem. Schindler never recovered financially after the war, and throughout his life depended on the financial support of the Jews he helped to save.

A sign proclaims the location of the Avenue of the Righteous. Although Israelis consider the Righteous Gentiles to be heroes deserving honor and financial support for the rest of their lives, Righteous Gentiles themselves are often modest, proclaiming that they only did what anyone would do.

thing does not merit a reward. Some have said that to give people awards for acting humanely implies that goodness is exceptional and evil acts are "normal."

When German rescuer Gitta Bauer heard that she was to receive a medal for her rescue work during the war, she called Ilse Baumgart, the person who had given testimony on her behalf, and expressed reservations. After all, Bauer said, she had not saved Baumgart for personal gain. Baumgart per-

suaded her to accept the Yad Vashem medal, saying, "You know, there are so few people in the world who know that not *all* Germans were bad."[110] Bauer's aunt, who sheltered Jews in her home in Amsterdam, was also honored.

Many Righteous Gentiles proudly display their medals and certificates from Yad Vashem. Some of them say that these honors have instilled pride in their children and grandchildren and have inspired them to continue the tradition of helping others. Recognition from Yad Vashem has helped to comfort family members who received awards on behalf of loved ones who died to save others.

Beyond their status as award recipients, rescuers have also been the focus of seminars and meetings. When he was chairman of the United States Holocaust Memorial Council in Washington, D.C., author and Auschwitz survivor Elie Wiesel called for an international conference on the subject of rescuers. "Faith in Humankind: Rescuers of Jews During the Holocaust," sponsored by the U.S. State Department, was held in September 1984.

Its organizers stressed the courage and humanity shown by an important minority during the Holocaust. Wiesel says that it is important to understand what makes the rescuers "different from their fellow citizens,"[111] willing to risk so much to save others, often strangers. By looking at their actions, we can all realize that much more could have been done than simply to stand by and give in to the Nazis, allowing evil to triumph.

The United States Holocaust Museum and Memorial in Washington, D.C., features exhibits that describe the acts of Righteous Gentiles. Among the items on display is a fishing boat of the type used by the Danes during their daring sea rescues in 1943.

In addition to being singled out for various honors, Righteous Gentiles have aroused the interest of scientists who want to learn more about human nature. Some

A Twelve-Year-Old Honors a Rescuer

The Jewish Foundation for the Righteous, based in New York City, has devoted itself to educational and charitable activities related to rescuers. One of its most important projects is to support needy rescuers. As of 1997, nearly thirteen hundred Christians in twenty-six countries were receiving checks from the foundation. Its Honor a Rescuer program enables individuals, synagogues, community organizations, schools, and other groups to be paired with a rescuer.

In 1997, when it was time for her bat mitzvah—an important celebration for Jewish girls—twelve-year-old Rebecca Marmor of Manlius, New York, decided to take part in this effort. The foundation sent her information about various rescuers, and she chose to send one thousand dollars that she had received in gifts to an eighty-four-year-old Polish woman, Irena Sendler.

During the Holocaust, Sendler helped to save twenty-five hundred children from the Warsaw ghetto, then hid them in Gentile homes. As a social worker, she used her position to provide food, medicine, and clothing for people in need. The network she worked with, the Zegota, also ran youth programs and helped young people to cope with the problems caused by the war. In an interview in the March 3, 1997, issue of *Family Circle*, Marmor explained, "When I read about Irena, I thought she was especially courageous and that's why I chose her."

have been the subject of research studies that compare rescuers with other people who either stood by and did nothing or who helped the Nazis.

In the introduction to *Rescuers: Portraits of Moral Courage in the Holocaust*, author Malka Drucker asks some of the questions that have kindled such interest:

> Who were these people who did not say, "That's not my problem"? Why were they different from others? Were they afraid? Why did they take such great risks? What has life been like for them since the war? Did they remain altruists? Have they been changed by their wartime experience? What did their deeds mean to them and their children?[112]

Drucker, who has interviewed more than one hundred rescuers from eleven different countries, concludes that these Gentiles shared "compassion, empathy, an intolerance of injustice, and an ability to endure risk beyond what one wants to imagine." In addition, they were able to identify with people who were being victimized. Says Drucker, "They did not distinguish between 'us' and 'them.'"[113]

Lessons for the Future

Although many rescuers remained silent about their activities after the war, the passage of time and various events have prompted more of them to speak out. The trial of Nazi war criminal Adolf Eichmann in 1961 was such an event. For years, Israeli intelligence agents had been searching for Eichmann before they finally found him in South America living under an assumed name. The trial, held in Jerusalem, was broadcast on television and radio. People

After hearing that some people refused to believe that the Holocaust happened, Irene Gut Opdyke dedicated her life to lecturing full time on the Holocaust.

around the world heard testimony from Holocaust survivors with knowledge of Eichmann's role in Nazi barbarism, as well as Eichmann's own damning testimony. Some were hearing about these horrors for the first time.

As people confronted the evil of the Nazi years, there was a renewed interest in the rescuers, the Righteous Gentiles, those who had acted humanely. These people had risked everything to help others, many of them strangers, and to uphold the highest human values. Righteous Gentiles were urged to discuss their experiences, to give others hope and be living examples of goodness.

Some rescuers came forward to make sure the Holocaust was not forgotten. In

Remembering a Heroic Diplomat

In 1992, the people of Yaotsu, Japan, dedicated a magnificent memorial to a native son, Sempo Sugihara. This peaceful monument, located along a mountain ridge, is called the Hill of Humanity.

During the 1930s, Sugihara was a Japanese consul based in Kovno, Lithuania. He defied the instructions of his government and issued thousands of transit visas to Jews who were desperately fleeing the Nazis. These Jews had permits to enter various countries around the world but needed transit visas. The visas Sugihara gave them allowed them to travel through Japan in order to reach their destinations.

The Japanese government banned him from issuing the visas not once but three times. Sugihara continued to write them, working from a hotel with his wife after the Russians invaded that region of Lithuania and closed down the Japanese consulate. As many as ten thousand people may have been saved by Sugihara's decision to follow his conscience. Sugihara did not regret what he had done, although he was dismissed from the diplomatic corps for his actions and spurned by people in his own country.

The memorial consists of 160 ceramic pipes of different sizes, symbolizing different countries of the world. The pipes are operated by computer and produce water, lights, and music in a setting of flowers, shrubs, and small trees. One of the trees at the monument was planted by a man whom Sugihara helped, Rabbi Zerah Warhaftig, the former Israeli religious affairs minister.

Sempo Sugihara issued thousands of visas to Jews fleeing Nazi persecution. A memorial is dedicated to him in Yaotsu, Japan.

1975, Polish rescuer Irene Gut Opdyke was living in California, having buried her painful wartime experiences. She received a letter in the mail from a group that was promoting so-called revisionist history. The group alleged that the Holocaust had never happened, that it was a lie concocted to arouse sympathy for Jews and arouse hostility toward Germans. Opdyke was enraged. In order to share her firsthand knowledge, she changed her life to lecture full-time on the Holocaust. She told author Eva Fogelman,

"I particularly want to educate the young. [With] every child I reach and change I am helping to change all of humanity."[114] Opdyke says that she receives wonderful letters from schoolchildren saying that her story has given them more courage to handle their own problems.

Miep Gies also shied away from the spotlight and had to be urged to tell her story. Her book, *Anne Frank Remembered*, moved many people and inspired a television movie and an Academy Award–winning documentary in 1996. Like many rescuers, Gies felt a moral duty to ensure that times like those "will never, never come again. It is for all of us ordinary people all over the world to see to it that they do not."[115]

German rescuer Helene Jacobs has also committed herself to educating people about the Holocaust. She believes that Christians must think deeply about what happened and take care that their religions do not promote anti-Semitic teachings or attitudes.

Ukrainian rescuer Helena Zahajkewycz Melnyczuk says, "We have to teach our children to love one another, to be their brother's keeper. The truth is that the war didn't change human nature, and if that war didn't change people, what can?"[116]

Authors Samuel and Pearl Oliner write:

The human potential for destructiveness and indifference that was so manifest [during World War II] overwhelms us with despair as we view its recurrence around the globe. The naggingly persistent question is, What can ordinary people do? Rescuers point the way. They were and are ordinary people. They were farmers and teachers, entrepreneurs and factory workers, rich and poor, parents and single people, Protestants and Catholics.[117]

These people continue to inspire and to teach through example. Among other things, they show that simply to know right from wrong is not enough. One must also act. Having witnessed great wrongs, despite grievous danger, these people took action; around them, 700 million others did not. In the words of Polish rescuer Jan Karski, "Everyone has a soul, a human conscience. We have an infinite capacity to choose between evil and good."[118] By choosing acts of goodness, the Righteous Gentiles preserved human decency in a time of infinite evil.

Notes

Introduction: Choosing Goodness

1. Quoted in Carol Rittner and Sondra Myers, *The Courage to Care: Rescuers of Jews During the Holocaust.* New York: New York University Press, 1986, p. 19.

2. Quoted in Rittner and Myers, *The Courage to Care*, p. x.

3. Gay Block and Malka Drucker, *Rescuers: Portraits of Moral Courage in the Holocaust.* New York: Holmes and Meier, 1992, p. 10.

4. Quoted in Bea Stadtler, *The Holocaust: A History of Courage and Resistance.* New York: Behrman House, 1973, p. 145.

5. Quoted in Samuel P. Oliner and Pearl M. Oliner, *The Altruistic Personality: Rescuers of Jews in Nazi Europe.* New York: Free Press, 1988, pp. 168–69.

6. Quoted in Oliner and Oliner, *The Altruistic Personality*, p. 169.

7. Quoted in Oliner and Oliner, *The Altruistic Personality*, p. 228.

8. Quoted in Rittner and Myers, *The Courage to Care*, p. 27.

9. Quoted in Philip Friedman, *Their Brother's Keeper.* New York: Holocaust Library, 1978, p. 14.

Chapter 1: Righteous Gentiles in Hitler's Germany

10. Quoted in Block and Drucker, *Rescuers*, p. 149.

11. Quoted in Block and Drucker, *Rescuers*, p. 150.

12. Quoted in Block and Drucker, *Rescuers*, p. 150.

13. Quoted in Eva Fogelman, *Conscience and Courage: Rescuers of Jews During the Holocaust.* New York: Doubleday, 1994, p. 62.

14. Quoted in Fogelman, *Conscience and Courage*, p. 47.

15. Quoted in Thomas Keneally, *Schindler's List.* New York: Simon & Schuster, 1982, p. 133.

16. Quoted in Keneally, *Schindler's List*, p. 173.

17. Quoted in Keneally, *Schindler's List*, p. 256.

18. Quoted in Friedman, *Their Brother's Keeper*, p. 97.

19. Martin Niemöller, *The Gestapo Defied*, London: William Hodge, 1941, p. 67.

20. Quoted in Yehuda Bauer, *A History of the Holocaust.* New York: Franklin Watts, 1982, p. 137.

21. Quoted in Block and Drucker, *Rescuers*, p. 146.

22. Quoted in Block and Drucker, *Rescuers*, p. 148.

Chapter 2: Righteous Gentiles in Poland and Czechoslovakia

23. Quoted in Vera Laska, ed., *Women of the Resistance and in the Holocaust.* Westport, CT: Greenwood Press, 1984, p. 280.

24. Quoted in Friedman, *Their Brother's Keeper*, p. 111.

25. Quoted in Block and Drucker, *Rescuers*, p. 186.

26. Quoted in Fogelman, *Conscience and*

Courage, p. 116.

27. Quoted in Fogelman, *Conscience and Courage*, p. 117.

28. Quoted in Fogelman, *Conscience and Courage*, p. 106.

29. Nelly S. Toll, *Behind the Secret Window: A Memoir of a Hidden Childhood During World War II*. New York: Dial Books, 1993, p. 34.

30. Quoted in Toll, *Behind the Secret Window*, p. 77.

31. Toll, *Behind the Secret Window*, p. 106.

32. Quoted in Block and Drucker, *Rescuers*, p. 207.

33. Quoted in Fogelman, *Conscience and Courage*, p. 93.

34. Quoted in Fogelman, *Conscience and Courage*, p. 93.

35. Fogelman, *Conscience and Courage*, p. 104.

Chapter 3: Righteous Gentiles in the Baltics and Ukraine

36. Quoted in Milton Meltzer, *Rescue: The Story of How Gentiles Saved Jews in the Holocaust*. New York: Harper & Row, 1988, p. 43.

37. Quoted in Friedman, *Their Brother's Keeper*, p. 22.

38. Quoted in Block and Drucker, *Rescuers*, p. 242.

39. Quoted in Block and Drucker, *Rescuers*, p. 242.

40. Quoted in Block and Drucker, *Rescuers*, p. 244.

41. Quoted in Block and Drucker, *Rescuers*, p. 238.

Chapter 4: Righteous Gentiles in Scandinavia and the Low Countries

42. Quoted in Peter Hellman, *Avenue of the Righteous*. New York: Atheneum, 1980, p. 28.

43. Quoted in Hellman, *Avenue of the Righteous*, p. 31.

44. Quoted in Hellman, *Avenue of the Righteous*, p. 37.

45. Quoted in Hellman, *Avenue of the Righteous*, p. 39.

46. Quoted in Hellman, *Avenue of the Righteous*, p. 37.

47. Quoted in Hellman, *Avenue of the Righteous*, p. 47.

48. Quoted in Ariel L. Bauminger, *Roll of Honor*. Tel Aviv: Hamenora Publishing House, 1971, pp. 70–72.

49. Miep Gies with Alison Leslie Gold, *Anne Frank Remembered: The Story of the Woman Who Helped to Hide the Frank Family*. New York: Simon & Schuster, 1987, p. 96.

50. Gies, *Anne Frank Remembered*, p. 157.

51. Quoted in Gies, *Anne Frank Remembered*, p. 159.

52. Gies, *Anne Frank Remembered*, p. 11.

53. Quoted in Rittner and Myers, *The Courage to Care*, p. 33.

54. Quoted in Fogelman, *Conscience and Courage*, p. 178.

55. Quoted in Friedman, *Their Brother's Keeper*, pp. 40–41.

56. Quoted in Stadtler, *The Holocaust*, p. 143.

57. Quoted in Leora Kahn and Rachel Hager, eds., *When They Came to Take My Father: Voices of the Holocaust*. New York: Arcade, 1996, p. 43.

58. Robert Goldston, *The Life and Death of Nazi Germany*. New York: Fawcett, 1967, p. 166.

Chapter 5: Righteous Gentiles in France

59. Quoted in Friedman, *Their Brother's Keeper*, p. 51.

60. Quoted in Meltzer, *Rescue*, p. 79.

61. Quoted in Rittner and Myers, *The Courage to Care*, p. 101.

62. Quoted in Philip Hallie, *Lest Innocent Blood Be Shed: The Story of the Village of Le

Chambon and How Goodness Happened There. New York: Harper & Row, 1979, p. 120.

63. Quoted in Hallie, *Lest Innocent Blood Be Shed*, p. 107.

64. Quoted in Rittner and Myers, *The Courage to Care*, p. 103.

65. Quoted in Rittner and Myers, *The Courage to Care*, p. 103.

66. Quoted in Hallie, *Lest Innocent Blood Be Shed*, p. 109.

67. Interviewed in "Weapons of the Spirit," a documentary film produced by Pierre Sauvage. New York: First Run Features, 1989.

68. Interviewed in Sauvage, "Weapons of the Spirit."

69. Quoted in Friedman, *Their Brother's Keeper*, p. 50.

70. Quoted in Stacy Cretzmeyer, *Your Name Is Renee: Ruth's Story as a Hidden Child.* Brunswick, ME: Biddle, 1994, p. 53.

71. Quoted in Cretzmeyer, *Your Name Is Renee*, p. 81.

72. Quoted in Cretzmeyer, *Your Name Is Renee*, p. 84.

73. Quoted in Hellman, *Avenue of the Righteous*, p. 121.

74. Quoted in Hellman, *Avenue of the Righteous*, p. 126.

75. Quoted in Hellman, *Avenue of the Righteous*, p. 133.

76. Quoted in Hellman, *Avenue of the Righteous*, p. 161.

77. Quoted in Howard Greenfeld, *The Hidden Children.* New York: Ticknor and Fields, 1993, p. 39.

Chapter 6: Righteous Gentiles in Italy

78. Quoted in Alexander Stille, *Benevolence and Betrayal: Five Italian Jewish Families Under Fascism.* New York: Simon & Schuster, 1991, p. 197 .

79. Susan Zuccotti, *Italians and the Holocaust: Persecution, Rescue, and Survival.* New York: Basic Books, 1987, p. 109.

80. Quoted in Stille, *Benevolence and Betrayal*, p. 201.

81. Quoted in Stille, *Benevolence and Betrayal*, p. 206.

82. Quoted in Stille, *Benevolence and Betrayal*, p. 211.

83. Quoted in J. P. Gallagher, *Scarlet Pimpernel of the Vatican.* New York: Coward, McCann, 1967, p. 62.

84. Quoted in Gallagher, *Scarlet Pimpernel*, p. 62.

85. Quoted in Gallagher, *Scarlet Pimpernel*, p. 63.

86. Quoted in Alexander Ramati, as told by Padre Rufino Niccacci, *The Assisi Underground.* New York: Stein and Day, 1978, p. 5.

87. Quoted in Ramati, *The Assisi Underground*, p. 5.

88. Quoted in Ramati, *The Assisi Underground*, p. 37.

89. Quoted in Stille, *Benevolence and Betrayal*, p. 233.

90. Zuccotti, *Italians and the Holocaust*, p. 227.

Chapter 7: Righteous Gentiles in Hungary, Romania, Bulgaria, and Yugoslavia

91. Quoted in Maxine B. Rosenberg, *Hiding to Survive: Stories of Jewish Children Rescued from the Holocaust.* New York: Houghton Mifflin, 1994, p. 86.

92. Quoted in Rosenberg, *Hiding to Survive*, p. 93.

93. Quoted in Elaine Landau, *We Survived the Holocaust*, New York: Franklin Watts, 1991, p. 113.

94. Quoted in Landau, *We Survived the Holocaust*, p. 113.

95. Quoted in Landau, *We Survived the Holocaust*, p. 115.

96. Quoted in Block and Drucker, *Rescuers*, p. 218.

97. Quoted in Block and Drucker, *Rescuers*, p. 218.

98. Quoted in Laska, *Women of the Resistance*, p. 107.

99. Quoted in Block and Drucker, *Rescuers*, p. 226.

100. Quoted in Block and Drucker, *Rescuers*, p. 226.

101. Quoted in "Raoul Wallenberg: Between the Lines," a documentary film produced by Bob Weis. Santa Monica, CA: Rhino Home Video, 1991.

102. Quoted in Frederick E. Werbell and Thurston Clarke, *Lost Hero: The Mystery of Raoul Wallenberg*. New York: McGraw-Hill, 1982, pp. 111–12.

103. Quoted in Meltzer, *Rescue*, p. 113.

104. Quoted in Meltzer, *Rescue*, p. 114.

105. Quoted in Kahn and Hager, *When They Came to Take My Father*, p. 12.

Epilogue: Beacons of Hope

106. Quoted in Block and Drucker, *Rescuers*, p. 101.

107. Quoted in Block and Drucker, *Rescuers*, p. 57.

108. Ramati, *The Assisi Underground*, p. 177.

109. Quoted in Ramati, *The Assisi Underground*, p. 179.

110. Quoted in Block and Drucker, *Rescuers*, p. 136.

111. Quoted in Rittner and Myers, *The Courage to Care*, p. xv.

112. Block and Drucker, *Rescuers*, p. 5.

113. Block and Drucker, *Rescuers*, p. 5.

114. Quoted in Fogelman, *Conscience and Courage*, p. 289.

115. Gies, *Anne Frank Remembered*, p. 12.

116. Quoted in Block and Drucker, *Rescuers*, p. 245.

117. Oliner and Oliner, *The Altruistic Personality*, p. 259.

118. Quoted in Block and Drucker, *Rescuers*, p. 172.

For Further Reading

David A. Adler, *We Remember the Holocaust.* New York: Henry Holt, 1989. In dramatic first-person anecdotes, Holocaust survivors describe Hitler's rise to power, life under the Nazis, the ghettos and concentration camps, and their lives after 1945.

Miriam Chaikin, *A Nightmare in History: The Holocaust, 1933–1945.* New York: Clarion, 1987. Reveals the way the Nazis set up their totalitarian regime in Germany and launched a war against the Jews while seizing territory throughout Europe.

Stacy Cretzmeyer, *Your Name Is Renee: Ruth's Story as a Hidden Child.* Brunswick, ME: Biddle, 1994. The dramatic story of a child who fled with her parents to southern France, where she was forced to assume a false identity and hide in various places to escape the Nazis.

Anne Frank, *Anne Frank: The Diary of a Young Girl.* New York: Doubleday, 1952. Frank was a German-Jewish refugee in occupied Holland who hid from the Nazis in an attic with her parents, sister, and four others. Her diary reveals the concerns, hopes, and dreams of an exuberant teenage girl trying to survive this harrowing era.

Miep Gies with Alison Leslie Gold, *Anne Frank Remembered: The Story of the Woman Who Helped to Hide the Frank Family.* New York: Simon & Schuster, 1987. The memoirs of the woman who helped to hide Jews, including the family of Anne Frank, during the Holocaust. Gies gives a vivid description of life in Holland during the five brutal years of Nazi occupation.

Howard Greenfeld, *The Hidden Children.* New York: Ticknor and Fields, 1993. Engrossing accounts of Jewish children forced to conceal their identities and/or hide in various private homes, orphanages, convents, and other religious institutions to avoid being killed by the Nazis. Shows the narrow escapes and hardships these children endured as they were cut off from their families, schools, friends, outdoor play, and other normal activities.

Elaine Landau, *We Survived the Holocaust.* New York: Franklin Watts, 1991. Sixteen Holocaust survivors from various countries recall life under Hitler, their struggle to live, and their postwar experiences. These courageous people were children and teenagers at the time when Nazism turned their lives upside down.

Elenore Lester, *Wallenberg: The Man in the Iron Web.* Englewood Cliffs, NJ: Prentice-Hall, 1982. A biography of the courageous Swede who worked tirelessly to save the Jews of Hungary during the last grim months of the Holocaust.

Milton Meltzer, *Rescue: The Story of How Gentiles Saved Jews in the Holocaust.* New York: Harper & Row, 1988. Profiles of individuals and groups throughout Germany and occupied Europe who worked to save Jews during the Holocaust.

Carol Rittner and Sondra Myers, *The Courage to Care: Rescuers of Jews During the Holocaust*. New York: New York University Press, 1986. Profiles of people and groups, such as villagers in the area of Le Chambon. Essays discuss the historical context of the war and explore why certain people acted with courage and compassion while others stood by or collaborated with the Nazis. Includes first-person accounts of those who rescued Jews and those whom they helped.

Jack Roberts, *Oskar Schindler*. San Diego: Lucent Books, 1996. A biography for young people about the famous factory owner who saved more than twelve hundred Jews in Poland during the Holocaust.

Barbara Rogasky, *Smoke and Ashes: The Story of the Holocaust*. New York: Holiday House, 1988. This overview of the history and political events of the Holocaust includes a section on Righteous Gentiles and anti-Nazi resistance.

Maxine B. Rosenberg, *Hiding to Survive: Stories of Jewish Children Rescued from the Holocaust*. New York: Houghton Mifflin, 1994. Fourteen moving first-person accounts of individuals who survived the Nazi horror in their homelands by hiding with non-Jewish families or in monasteries, convents, orphanages, and other places.

Seymour Rossel, *The Holocaust*. New York: Franklin Watts, 1981. A readable account of Hitler's rise to power and the years from 1933 to 1945 as the Nazis swept across Europe.

Arnold P. Rubin, *The Evil That Men Do: The Story of the Nazis*. New York: Julian Messner, 1977. Written for young adults; shows how the Nazis grew into a large, powerful party that used propaganda and police power to control millions of Europeans in order to carry out Hitler's agenda of conquest and racial/ethnic hatred.

Victoria Sherrow, *Cities at War: Amsterdam*. New York: Macmillan, 1992. Describes life in Holland during the harsh five-year Nazi occupation and the valiant resistance and rescue efforts carried out by citizens in this tolerant, peace-loving nation.

Bea Stadtler, *The Holocaust: A History of Courage and Resistance*. New York: Behrman House, 1973. Written to help young people understand the Holocaust, with emphasis on Jewish leaders and resistance; profiles of Jews and Gentiles who resisted the Nazis.

Gail B. Stewart, *The Warsaw Ghetto*. San Diego: Lucent Books, 1995. A detailed look at daily life in the Warsaw ghetto, including resistance and the ghetto uprising. Numerous quotations and first-person accounts in letters, diaries, autobiographies, documents, and newspapers, among others.

Corrie Ten Boom, with John and Elizabeth Sherrill, *The Hiding Place*. Boston: G. K. Hall, 1973. A Dutch rescuer describes how she and her fellow church members resisted the Nazis and hid Jews.

Nelly S. Toll, *Behind the Secret Window: A Memoir of a Hidden Childhood During World War II*. New York: Dial Books, 1993. Author and artist Nelly Toll describes her life in hiding with her mother in the home of a Catholic couple in occupied Poland. Illustrated with vivid watercolors Toll painted as a child during the Holocaust.

Irving Werstein, *That Denmark Might Live: The Saga of the Danish Resistance in World War II*. Philadelphia: Macrae Smith, 1967. The story of resistance in Denmark after the Nazi invasion in April 1940. Shows the government refusal to cooperate with the Nazis and how citizens used sabotage, strikes, spying, and other means to defeat the invaders along with a massive rescue effort that saved nearly all the Jews in Denmark.

Works Consulted

Stanislaw Adler, *In the Warsaw Ghetto: 1940–1943*. Jerusalem: Yad Vashem, 1982. Description of daily life and the struggle to survive in the Warsaw ghetto where tens of thousands of Jews were forced to live without enough food, sanitation, and adequate health care facilities. Shows how people lived, worked, ran schools, and courageously tried to resist the Nazis.

Inge Auerbacher, *I Am a Star: Child of the Holocaust*. New York: Prentice-Hall, 1985. Auerbacher, born in Germany in 1934, gives a first-person account of her life as a child during the Holocaust. She was one of about one hundred children (out of more than fifteen thousand) to survive the Theresienstadt concentration camp in Czechoslovakia.

Yehuda Bauer, *A History of the Holocaust*. New York: Franklin Watts, 1982. Describes the political, social, and economic background of Hitler's rise to power and detailed coverage of the years 1933–1945 as the Nazis swept across the continent intent on destroying European Jewry.

Ariel L. Bauminger, *Roll of Honor*. Tel Aviv: Hamenora Publishing House, 1971. Dramatic stories of rescues throughout Europe that saved Jewish men, women, and children from the Nazis.

Norman H. Baynes, ed., *The Speeches of Adolf Hitler*. New York: Howard Fertig, 1969. A collection of Hitler's speeches covering his rise to power in the Nazi Party through his death in 1945.

Mary Berg, *Warsaw Ghetto Diary*. New York: L. B. Fischer, 1945. An engrossing and moving account of life in the ghetto from the perspective of a sixteen-year-old girl.

Gay Block and Malka Drucker, *Rescuers: Portraits of Moral Courage in the Holocaust*. New York: Holmes and Meier, 1992. A collection of first-person accounts of people throughout Europe who have been honored as Righteous Gentiles. Text includes rescue efforts in various countries. Essays explore the nature of helping behavior and the moral choices Gentiles made during the Holocaust.

Lucy S. Dawidowicz, *The War Against the Jews, 1933–1945*. New York: Holt, Rinehart, and Winston, 1975. Informative look at how Hitler used the larger war of conquest to wage his war of hatred against civilian Jewish men, women, and children.

Bernt Engelmann, *In Hitler's Germany: Everyday Life in the Third Reich*. New York: Knopf, 1986. A look at how individual Germans became bystanders, collaborators, or resisters during the war by an author who worked with a rescue and resistance network.

Eva Fogelman, *Conscience and Courage: Rescuers of Jews During the Holocaust*. New York: Doubleday, 1994. Detailed profiles of rescuers, with first-person narrative, along with an analysis of the qualities and circumstances that led Gentiles to become rescuers.

Philip Friedman, *Their Brother's Keeper*. New York: Holocaust Library, 1978. Readable, dramatic accounts of numerous individuals and groups throughout Europe who saved Jews during the Holocaust.

J. P. Gallagher, *Scarlet Pimpernel of the Vatican*. New York: Coward, McCann, 1967. Biography of Father Hugh O'Flaherty, an Irish priest who hid Jews and Allied prisoners of war in the Vatican and led a rescue network in Rome.

Martin Gilbert, *The Holocaust*. New York: Holt, Rinehart, and Winston, 1985. Thorough, well-documented historical account.

Martin Gilbert, *The Macmillan Atlas of the Holocaust*. London: Michael Joseph, 1982. Chronological history of the Holocaust showing major events against the backdrop of the war throughout Europe; numerous maps.

Robert Goldston, *The Life and Death of Nazi Germany*. New York: Fawcett, 1967. Readable account of the Nazi rise to power through the end of the war; quotes from Hitler's speeches and writings.

Philip Hallie, *Lest Innocent Blood Be Shed: The Story of the Village of Le Chambon and How Goodness Happened There*. New York: Harper & Row, 1979. Based on interviews with the religious leaders and citizens of Le Chambon, Hallie describes the large-scale effort that saved thousands of lives, mostly children.

Peter Hellman, *Avenue of the Righteous*. New York: Atheneum, 1980. Detailed stories about several rescuers in France, Belgium, and Poland; describes their activities during the war and their lives and the lives of the people they saved since 1945.

Leora Kahn and Rachel Hager, eds., *When They Came to Take My Father: Voices of the Holocaust*. New York: Arcade, 1996. Firsthand accounts by men and women from various countries who survived the Holocaust. They include concentration camp survivors, people who fled to safety, and others who remained in hiding during the war.

Thomas Keneally, *Schindler's List*. New York: Simon & Schuster, 1982. Biography of the businessman who saved more than twelve hundred Jews in Poland during the Holocaust. The book on which the acclaimed Steven Spielberg movie of the same name is based.

Vera Laska, ed., *Women of the Resistance and in the Holocaust*. Westport, CT: Greenwood Press, 1984. A detailed look at women during the Holocaust, with many first-person accounts and essays; edited by a former member of the Czech resistance and concentration camp survivor.

Donald Lowrie, *The Hunted Children*. New York: W. W. Norton, 1963. Describes the perilous life of children in hiding during the Holocaust and the problems caused by hiding one's identity as well as having to live underground.

Kati Marton, *Wallenberg*. New York: Random House, 1982. Acclaimed biography by a Hungarian-born author of the Swedish diplomat who saved tens of thousands of Hungarian Jews from the Nazis. Last chapters trace Wallenberg's movements in the Soviet prison system after the war.

Judith Miller, *One by One by One: Facing the Holocaust*. New York: Simon & Schuster, 1990. Interviews and first-person accounts show the many ways in which individuals and their families suffered from the horrors of the Holocaust.

Martin Niemöller, *The Gestapo Defied*. London: William Hodge, 1941. A memoir by the German Lutheran pastor who was imprisoned for protesting Nazism and later worked for reconciliation between Christians and Jews.

Samuel P. Oliner and Pearl M. Oliner, *The Altruistic Personality: Rescuers of Jews in Nazi Europe*. New York: Free Press, 1988. Results of a psychological study comparing the backgrounds and traits of rescuers with those of nonrescuers.

Alexander Ramati, as told by Padre Rufino Niccacci, *The Assisi Underground*. New York: Stein and Day, 1978. Fascinating account of rescues by a group organized by Catholic clergy in Assisi. Written by a Holocaust survivor, based on extensive interviews with a priest who led the group.

"Raoul Wallenberg: Between the Lines," film documentary produced by Bob Weis, written and directed by Karin Altmann. Santa Monica, CA: Rhino Home Video, 1991. Dramatic portrayal of the life and heroic rescue work of the Swedish diplomat. Explores various diplomatic and individual efforts to find Wallenberg after his arrest by the Soviets in 1945.

Carol Rittner and John K. Roth, eds., *Different Voices: Women and the Holocaust*. New York: Paragon House, 1993. Experiences of women of different ages; includes stories of rescue and many firsthand accounts of life in hiding or in concentration camps.

Leesha Rose, *The Tulips Are Red*. New York: A. S. Barnes, 1978. Rose's account of her life as a young Jewish woman in occupied Holland who managed to elude the Nazis and join Righteous Gentiles and other Jews in a rescue and resistance network.

Margaret L. Rossiter, *Women in the Resistance*. New York: Praeger, 1986. Focuses on how women in various European countries rescued Jews and others and resisted the Nazis during the Holocaust.

Andre Stein, *Quiet Heroes: True Stories of the Rescue of Jews by Christians in Nazi-Occupied Holland*. Toronto: Lester & Orpen Dennys, 1988. Dramatic stories of how a variety of people took action to save Dutch Jews and refugees from the Nazis from 1940 to 1945.

Alexander Stille, *Benevolence and Betrayal: Five Italian Jewish Families Under Fascism*. New York: Simon & Schuster, 1991. Detailed and moving account of the fate of five Jewish families living in various parts of Italy during the Holocaust.

Nechama Tec, *When Light Pierced the Darkness: Christian Rescue of Jews in Occupied Poland*. New York: Oxford University Press, 1986. Stories about groups and individuals from all walks of life who risked death to save Jews in Poland.

"Weapons of the Spirit," film documentary written and produced by Pierre Sauvage. Distributed by First Run Features, 1989. Through photographs, historical film footage, and interviews, filmmaker Sauvage tells the inspiring story of the French rescuers of Le Chambon.

Frederick E. Werbell and Thurston Clarke, *Lost Hero: The Mystery of Raoul Wallenberg*. New York: McGraw-Hill, 1982. A vivid account of Wallenberg's unique heroism during World War II and his mysterious disappearance during the cold war years that followed.

Jacqueline Wolf, *Take Care of Josette: A Memoir in Defense of Occupied France*. New York: Franklin Watts, 1981. A dramatic story of French rescuers.

Leni Yahil, *The Holocaust: The Fate of European Jewry*. New York: Oxford University Press, 1990. Considered one of the best, most comprehensive works of Holocaust literature, based on more than twenty years of research. Three detailed chapters cover rescue efforts, particularly during the end of the war.

Susan Zuccotti, *Italians and the Holocaust: Persecution, Rescue, and Survival*. New York: Basic Books, 1987. A well-documented account of the fate of Italian Jews during the war; how social and political conditions enabled 85 percent of them to survive.

Index

Picture Credits

Cover photo: Rijksinstituut voor Oorlogsdocumentatie, courtesy of USHMM Photo Archives

AP/Wide World Photos, 17, 21, 84

Archive Photos/Bernard Gotfryd, 50

Archive Photos/Reuters, 85

Zdenko Bergl, courtesy of USHMM Photo Archives, 69

Bibliotheque Historique de la Ville de Paris, courtesy of USHMM Photo Archives, 58

Gay Block and Malta Drucker, courtesy of USHMM Photo Archives, 27, 28, 40, 52, 54, 92

Bundesarchiv, courtesy of USHMM Photo Archives, 36

Corbis-Bettmann, 57, 71

Ferenc Flamm, courtesy of USHMM Photo Archives, 83

Frihedsmuseet, courtesy of USHMM Photo Archives, 55

Hoover Institution, courtesy of USHMM Photo Archives, 38

Hungarian National Museum, Photo Archives, courtesy of USHMM Photo Archives, 77

Jewish Historical Institute, courtesy of USHMM Photo Archives, 30

Jack Lewin, courtesy of USHMM Photo Archives, 62

Library of Congress, 9

Frank Morgens, courtesy of USHMM Photo Archives, 63

John W. Mosenthal, courtesy of USHMM Photo Archives, 33

National Archives, 31, 68

National Archives, courtesy of USHMM Photo Archives, 16

Papers of André and Magda Trocmé/Nelly Trocmé Hewett and the Swarthmore College Peace Collection, courtesy of USHMM Photo Archives, 60

Peter Newark's Historical Pictures, 25

About the Author

Victoria Sherrow holds B.S. and M.S. degrees from Ohio State University. Among her writing credits are numerous stories and articles, six books of fiction, and more than forty works of nonfiction for children and young adults. Her recent books have explored such topics as public education in America, the role of the media in U.S. elections, and the U.S. health care system. Sherrow lives in Connecticut with her husband, Peter Karoczkai, and their three children.